MIMESIS
INTERNATIONAL

W0017064

ASIAN PHILOSOPHICAL TEXTS

No. 3

Book series edited by Roman Paşca (Kyoto University, Japan) and Takeshi Morisato

VANISHING SUBJECTIVITY

Flower, Shame, and Direct Cultivation in Asian Philosophies

Edited by
Takeshi Morisato and Roman Paşca

MIMESIS
INTERNATIONAL

© 2021 – MIMESIS INTERNATIONAL – MILAN
www.mimesisinternational.com
e-mail: info@mimesisinternational.com

Isbn: 9788869773341
Book series: *Asian Philosophical Texts,* n. 3

© MIM Edizioni Srl
P.I. C.F. 02419370305

CONTENTS

INTRODUCTION

In Miyazawa Kenji's story *The Restaurant of Many Orders*, two gentlemen from the city have no choice but to enter the "fine brick building" with a strange sign, "Western Restaurant Wildcat House" (西洋料理店・山猫軒). They have lost their mountain guide who knows the ways of the wild and their hunting dogs seem to have completely lost their sense of direction in the middle of dark woods. Also since these gentlemen are not equipped with any sense of value beyond the crudest form of materialism (and that is certainly obvious from the fact that they have embraced the idea of killing animals for sport), their hunger has easily overcome their reason in entering this strange place.

Our Anglo-European readers, especially if we have any sense of quality beyond the confines of capitalism, may refrain from making the same mistake. Imagine going to the countryside of Guangdong, China or whichever part of the Kanto region in Japan. When we cannot find any business facilities for miles, we come across a small building that has a sign, "Western Restaurant" (西洋料理店). We have to be desperate in finding anything to satiate our hunger or lower our expectations to the bare minimum, hoping to find anything that might remind of us our "home." The same goes for Asian readers in Europe. They would not feel comfortable going into a facility with a ridiculous sign, "Asian Diner." If they have no choice but to enter one of these fusion restaurants that obliterate any conventional distinctions like Chinese, Korean, or Japanese, they will probably look at the menu and see what kind of dishes they are risking their lives for. It is highly doubtful that they would find anything there that would remind them of their specific culinary traditions from their home countries.

When this playful analogy is applied to the condition in which we prepare a philosophy course in academia or engage in an editorial process of compiling a text for the intellectual audience in Europe or North America, we face a serious problem. If we would never eat a food that is described as "European" or "Asian," and also if we would strive to know more specifics about each dish before touching it, why should we read or write a book that says "Asian philosophy"? Why should we take a course or listen to a lecture that says "Asian philosophy" at universities (without questioning the audacity [if not the stupidity] of someone who came up with the course title)? Or most importantly, what are the conditions in which this terrible generalization has become a necessity for us?

Miyazawa Kenji's tale shows that the Wildcat House is not a real building where you can order what you like to satiate your hunger. Nor is it designed to protect your body from the hostile environment. It is rather the site of internal reflection where we can realize how what we are doing to animals and the world outside us is eventually what we are doing to ourselves. This place of self-awareness comes upon us when we are incapable of recognizing the richness of our natural environment, and also when the wealth of knowledge stored in various intellectual traditions escapes our impoverished intellect, and we find ourselves entering it without asking too many serious questions.

Most universities in Europe seem to be downsizing their philosophy programs (along with other vital disciplines in the field of the humanities). If not, they are certainly not expanding it to include more courses that would explore the vast domain of the Asian philosophical traditions. A few departments may speak of diversity and cultural inclusion by running global, intercultural, or world philosophy programs. But these fringe activities usually mean that they have a single professor teaching an entire history of a single intellectual tradition (like Chinese, Indian, or Islamic philosophy) if they are not expected to teach a course on "Asian philosophy."

Of course this is preposterous. It would be reckless to assign a single professor to teach the entire history of European philosophy and expect her to carry out decent research on any topics that pertain to this tradition on her own. We would not expect her to find colleagues at the same department who are genuinely interested in her work either. Then why do we do this to the specialists of Asian philosophies when we, for instance, expect a single instructor to teach the entire intellectual and cultural history of China or India? How could they possibly teach the whole history, literature, philosophy, etc., in relation to each of these loosely defined geopolitical regions? If we bother to know the outline of Chinese or Indian philosophy, it would be culturally offensive and politically incorrect to hire an academic per discipline (let alone hiring one instructor to cover all under one and only "Asian philosophy" course!).

The current "funding application" scheme in academia recklessly tends towards specialization in the preestablished context of European (mostly analytic and occasionally continental) philosophy. What is required to establish the field of non-Anglo-European philosophy is not a series of specialized projects but the intersubjective examinations that outline the entire field of a single intellectual tradition. It will call for a number of translation projects that publish a fraction of its literary output, countless introductory essays that simply locate hitherto neglected thinkers in the heuristic framework of world philosophies, and they may not be cited by other articles in today's leading philosophy journals for years to come. Since academia maintains its quality and dominant discourse through the peer-review system, the voice of the minorities will always be marginalized, and naturally, most publishers in Europe and North America hesitate to invest in books on world philosophies.

In this desolate field of academic philosophy, we have no choice but to name the site of our internal reflection "Asian philosophical texts." We hope that there will be a day in which we realize that the term "Asian" is as unessential as "European" when talking about philosophical ideas. We hope that our readers will immediately ask us "which part of Asia" and "which historical period of a specific intellectual tradition" we are talking about. Just as women's suffrage in Europe is self-evident today, we fight for the truth that the notion of philosophy should be entitled to various intellectual traditions in Asia and beyond. It is not possible to achieve this end with one book just as the restaurant with many orders did not succeed in converting the hearts-and-minds of the gentlemen. However, "the two gentlemen's faces, scrunched up like balled-up paper, even when they went back to Tokyo, even when they took a bath, never returned to normal." We are confident that this book will too leave a mark in our ways of living a philosophic life, thus playing a small part in bringing closer the day of reckoning for philosophers.

The first part of this volume, this "restaurant of many orders" of ours, consists of three articles which take us from China to Japan and then to Central Asia, from Mencius and his concept of shame to Zeami and his theory of subjectivity and then to Yūsuf Balasaguni and his philosophy of language.

In "The Mencian Concept of Chi-Shame", Yu Yihsoong analyzes the concept of "shame" in a Confucian context starting from the observation that historical investigations have a tendency to hold that the Chinese concept is more internalized than the term in English. Noting that there are in fact two different words used to express the concept of shame—*xiu* 羞 and *chi* 恥, not exactly interchangeable — Yu discusses the differences between them and then, drawing on Martha Nussbaum and Bernard Williams' understanding of shame and guilt, performs a careful and incisive dissection of *chi*-shame to show that it indicates a developed moral emotion which unites assessments of self-image and responsibility into a single philosophical reflection. Through a thorough examination of references to shame in texts such as the *Analects* or the *Mengzi*, Yu Yihsoong demonstrates that *chi*-shame is both internal and ethical, that is it already inclusive of guilt, and that it may be understood as the equivalent to Mencius' designation of the "heart of *xiu*-shame and disdain." In other words, a proper understanding of *chi*-shame points to the inseparability of shame and guilt, and thus the concept should be interpreted as the unity of both terms. In this sense, *chi*-shame is extremely significant for the process of moral self-cultivation, which is indispensible for realizing the Confucian idea of moral righteousness.

In "The Flower as Encountering: the Ultimate Goal for the Emptiness of an Actor's Subjectivity in Zeami's Performance Theory," Taisuke Ueno investigates Zeami's (世阿弥元清, ca. 1363 – ca. 1443) performance theory from a philosophical perspective in an attempt to identify the constitutive elements of the Nō actor's subjectivity, and the process through which it is achieved. Ueno first discusses Nishihira's interpretation that Zeami argued for a double-layered subjectivity, i.e., that after the Nō actor achieves a high-level performance *unconsciously*, he then revisits his performace technique *consciously*, thus renewing his subjectivity. Noting that while Nishihira's view does indeed clarify the general frame of Zeami's thought from the perspective of Western philosophical concepts, Ueno shows that it also tends to relegate into insignificance its indigenous, "unenlightened" facet, namely its relation with religious rituals and Zeami's account of the origins of Nō. Examining references to the actor's performance and the concept of "flower" in several of Zeami's texts, Ueno proposes the tension between *wo suru* ("performing the character intentionally") and *ni naru* ("becoming the character unconsciously") as a possible framework for understanding the dialectical relation between the development and vanishment of subjectivity in the Nō actor. In his conclusions, Ueno suggests that the actor—and spectators, for that matter—needs to eliminate his subjectivity in order to allow Nō to come into existence, arguing that although we usually think that the actor plays the Nō performance, it is in fact the Nō that manifests itself through the fulfillment of the actor's performance as if it were vitalized when his subjectivity disappears.

In "Topology of Balasaguni's Kutadgu Bilig: Thinking the Between," Onur Karamercan focuses on the philosophical dimension of *Kutadgu Bilig*, a poetic work of Yūsuf Balasaguni, an 11th century Central Asian thinker, poet, and statesman. Karamercan pays special attention to the meaning of betweenness and, in the first step of his argument, discusses the hermeneutic and topological implications of the between, distingushing the dynamic sense of betweenness from a static sense of in-betweenness. He then moves on to analyze Balasaguni's notion of language, which he interprets as an early critique of the instrumental account of language and, by examining several selected fragments from *Kutadgu Bilig*, illustrates Balasaguni's designation of language as an inexhaustible phenomenon. In the process, he also points to the possible parallels between Balasaguni's and Heidegger's ideas of language. In the final section of the article, building on his argument, Karamercan thematizes the margins of Turkic languages and of Islamic philosophy, suggesting that they need to be reexamined. He problematizes the very meaning of Asia itself by decentering what he calls "its internal

East–West antagonism" and puts forth instead a framework based on in-betweenness reinterpreted from a topological perspective, proposing it as an alternative view which might help us make sense of the hermeneutic neighborhoods of Asian philosophies.

The second part of the volume completes the menu with four translations from Asian philosophical texts, accompanied by commentary and notes. Diana Yüksel translates Book 16 (*Chapch'e* 雑著, "Miscellaneous") of Korean poet and philosopher Kim Sisŭp's *Mewŏldangmunjip* 梅月堂文集, a sample of his vast knowledge of Confucian classics, but also of his insight into Buddhist and Daoist teachings as well as his flexible attitude towards all thought forms. Roman Paşca translates sections 7 through 16 from Japanese thinker Andō Shōeki's text *Taijokan* 大序巻 ("The Great Introduction"), his last work, which contains *in nuce* all the major themes of his philosophy, from his view of nature to his rather radical understanding of language. Rossa Ó Muireartaigh translates a less-known text by Kyoto school philosopher Tanabe Hajime, "On Confucianist Ontology" (*Jukyōteki sonzairon ni tsuite* 儒教的存在論に就いて), originally published in 1928, an essay in which Tanabe explores the cosmology of Confucianism through a reading of the *I-Ching*, one of the official five classics of Ancient China. Takeshi Morisato and Kyle Shuttleworth collaborate to translate the first two sections of Chapter 1 of Japanese contemporary philosopher Kimura Motomori's book "The Form of Beauty" (*Bi no katachi* 美のかたち), published in 1941, in which he discusses the problematic of art as expression.

Compiling and editing this third volume in the Asian Philosophical Texts book series has been a labor of love (and pain) for us the editors. In these uncertain times of havoc-wreaking pandemic, in an almost discouragingly harsh academe, isolated and separated by continents and time zones, what brought us together and kept us going was the shared ambition to create a locus of reflection, a place where philosophical ideas from different traditions and eras can meet and join into a polyvocal, fruitful dialogue. We hope we managed to create such a place, or at least lay the foundations for it. We would not have been able to do this without the generous help of many friends and colleagues, who offered advice, moral support and encouragement along the way. We thank all of them, especially Pierre Bonneels at the

Research Center for East Asian Studies (EASt) at Université libre de Bruxelles (ULB), and Taisuke Ueno and Alexandra Mustățea at the Research Institute for Japanese Studies (RIJS) at Kanda University of International Studies, for joining us in this project and for continuing to walk on the same path with us. The whole book series started as a spinoff of the Asian Philosophical Texts conference, which we organized for the first time in 2018 as part of the academic collaboration effort between EASt at ULB and RIJS at KUIS, and which we plan to continue to organize in the future as well. Our heartfelt gratitude goes to RIJS for also covering a significant portion of the publication costs for this project.

ESSAYS

Yu Yihsoong

THE MENCIAN CONCEPT OF CHI-SHAME

Ruth Benedict famously made a distinction between "shame" and "guilt cultures" in order to identify the differences between Japanese and American ethical views in the 1940s. Since then, many scholars have asked the question of whether or not the sense of shame could provide a ground for an internalized morality. Benedict's rendering of shame essentially gives a reaction to an external criticism base on the feelings of embarrassment, while guilt in contrast is the internalized conviction of sin.[1] Keiichi Sakuta, then, responded to Benedict's definitions with an analysis of the protagonist's inner monologue in *No Longer Human* (*Ningen Shikkaku* 人間失格) in the 1950s. He argued that a shame could be private to an individual but also guide us to develop an ethically ideal self, which prevents the individual from succumbing to social pressures.[2] Benedict's shame—guilt distinction also led to another question: Does shame play a healthier role than guilt in developing morality or vice versa? This is not a surprising response to Benedict's idea given that her distinction was eventually applied to identify Greek and modern views on ethics in the field of philosophy. Bernard Williams, for instance, argues in his study of Homer's classics that shame can be positive since it can not only structure one's ethical identity, but also enables oneself to be realistic about one's moral luck. Also, without shame, a moral self, which is constructed by the sense of guilt, would be characterless since guilt requires the self to obey moral principles without paying attention

---

1   Ruth Benedict, *The Chrysanthemum and The Sword* (United States of America: Houghton Mifflin Company, 1989), 225.

2   Keiichi Sakuta, 'A Reconsideration of the Culture of Shame', trans. Kimiko Yagi and Meridith Mckinney, *Review of Japanese Culture and Society* 1, no. 1 (1986): 32–39.

to any particular qualifications or conditions.[3] Williams's analysis of shame, in this manner, turned the general impression of "shame culture" into a positive one and thereby, inspired further historical and cultural studies that paid special attention to the function of shame in the making of civilizations.

Sinologists naturally followed Williams's step. This is a matter of course since Chinese ethics alongside Japanese *rinrigaku* had been identified with its embeddedness in a shame culture at this point of history. The most notable studies are done by Heiner Roetz, Bryan W. Van Norden, Jane Geaney, and Bongrae Seok.[4] All of these scholars have relied on the exegesis of the pre-Qin Confucian classics and more or less unanimously concluded that "shame" in Chinese culture is creative because it plays the role of developing self-esteem, rather than passively defending it from public criticisms. The differences of their takes lie in the question of how they have distinguished semantic nuances of the term and interpreted various metaphors of Chinese senses of shame as they translated them into English. Indeed, their comparative studies are quite sophisticated and even convinced many scholars of Chinese philosophy of its validity. However, I argue that they have all failed to recognize that there are two terms in Chinese that signify the concept of "shame": *xiu* 羞 and *chi* 恥; and their meanings are not exactly interchangeable. For the sake of clarity, I will occasionally refer to them as "*xiu*-shame" and "*chi*-shame" in this chapter. The purpose of this paper is to show that these specialists of ancient Chinese philosophy have failed to recognize the following two points: (1) the term, *chi*, carries an implication of "guilt" and (2) it signals a developed moral feeling, the feeling that is reducible

---

3   Bernard Williams, *Shame and Necessity* (Berkeley: University of California Press, 1993), 93–94.

4   Heiner Roetz, *Confucian Ethics of the Axial Age* (Albany: State University of New York Press, 1993); Bryan W. Van Norden, "The Emotion of Shame and the Virtue of Righteousness in Mencius," *Dao: A Journal of Comparative Philosophy* 2, no. 1 (2002): 45–77; Jane Geaney, "Moral Boundaries: Shame in Early Confucianism," *Philosophy East and West* 54, no. 2 (2004): 113–42; Bongrae Seok, "Moral Psychology of Shame in Early Confucian Philosophy," in *Reconceptualizing Confucian Philosophy in the 21st Century*, ed., X Yao (Singapore: Springer Nature Singapore Pte Ltd. and Higher Education Press, 2017), 117–49.

neither to the concept of guilt nor that of shame as understood in reference to the Anglo-European intellectual tradition.

R. E. Lamb argues that in English, the term "guilt" necessarily implies a feeling of responsibility in an agent while the term "shame" does not. For instance, we feel guilty when we think about a terrible thing that happened to a thing or a person; and this is done with a knowledge that had we done something, this tragic situation could have been avoided. There is a series of self-reflections towards the other and the sense of responsibility that self has contributed to the end result. But when we blush as we are overpowered by a feeling of shame, it happens against our will or desires and certainly does not require any reflections over this immediate emotional response. This means that shame points at our feeling that our self-image is, in one way or another, put into a question. However, according to Lamb, guilt does not have to bring up this self-image or involuntary emotional response because it can simply confine itself to a rational judgment over the agent's action. For instance, a vigilante can feel proud for who s/he is (that is to say s/he is beyond shame) and at the same time guilty (because his or her action does not fulfill the ethical mandate of following the law).[5] *Xiu* in Chinese refers to any kind of embarrassment as the English term, "shame," does. However, the *chi*-shame refers to a specific kind of embarrassment since it must be about the ethical character of one's action or self-image, thus necessarily implying that the moral agent is feeling responsible for a certain state of affairs.[6] That is to say, *chi*-shame always implies both guilt and shame regardless of the fact that it is translated as "shame."

---

5   Lamb has identified three hard facts about shame: "(i) The range of types of things about which it is possible to feel ashamed far exceeds the range of types of things about which it is possible to feel guilty. But also, (ii) It is analytically true that: If S feels guilty about x then S believes, rightly or wrongly (also rationally or irrationally), that he is in some measure responsible for x. (iii) It is not analytically true that: If S feels ashamed of x then S believes he is responsible for x." R.E. Lamb, "Guilt, Shame, and Morality," *Philosophy and Phenomenological Research* 43, no. 3 (1983): 335–36.

6   Shao-Ming Chen has identified four main terms to refer to the experience of shame in Chinese, and they do not share exactly the same implications. The table below is my translation of his conclusion, the original is in Shao-Ming Chen, "A Phenomenological Analysis of Shame," *Philosophical Research*, no. 12 (2006): 103.

The term, *chi* 恥, denotes the emotional state of a moral agent where her ethical self-image is called into question, and simultaneously, her self-awareness that she is responsible for the things or events that have led to the very questioning. In reference to a single instance of embarrassment, depending on calling it *chi*- or *xiu*-shame, we can expect different responses from a person. Consider the following example: "John's love letter was revealed by his friend to others in class." If the description of his response to the situation is that "he felt ashamed in the sense of *xiu*,"[7] then it implies that John was simply embarrassed about the revelation of his secret. This notion of *xiu*-shame in Chinese would be in line with the conventional interpretation of shame in English. But if the description is to state that "he felt ashamed in the sense of *chi*,"[8] then what is suggested here is that John was ethically embarrassed about the fact that he trusted a deceitful friend.

Indeed, shame and guilt are not always exclusive to each other as Lamb (among others) argues. The problem is that our emotional state always gives a mixture of various feelings. As Michael Stocker has indicated, a wrongdoing can evoke shame, just as a violation of an ideal self-image can evoke guilt.[9] However, in terms of semantics,

Categories Factors	Xiu (羞)	Kui (愧)	Chi (恥)	Ru (辱)
Model	None	Subjective	Subjective	Passive
Quality	Neutral	Failure	Guilty	Injured
Related Person	People on the scene	The one who is expectant Competitor	Intimate Victim	Enemy Intimate
Reaction	Escape Adaption	Escape Improve	Escape Correction	Escape Improve Revenge

7   In Chinese: "他感到害羞."
8   In Chinese: "他感到可恥."
9   Stocker reviewed the studies by Martha Nussbaum, Herbert Morris, Gerhart Piers, and Bernard Williams, and concluded that all of them fail to give a clear-cut distinction of shame and guilt, since both can mutually elicit each other in one's feelings; and thus he suggests that the consideration of morality must include self-evaluation and act-evaluation together. My revelation of the function of Chi-shame shares the same view as his suggestion in general. See Michael Stocker, "Shame and Guilt," ed., Paul Bloomfield (New York: Oxford University Press, 2008), 292–93.

there is always a lucid and determinate distinction between two terms of shame and guilt in English. The Chinese term, *chi*, clearly unites the emotions of shame and guilt into one concept. This is to say that we cannot understand this moral feeling with the binary distinction of shame and guilt but its emotional content as a shame (and not guilt) must be more developed or intellectually engaging than the concept of shame that we usually visualize in English; and at the same time, as the term shame is not reducible to the term, guilt, in both languages, its function must also be differentiated from the sense of guilt.

A close analysis of *chi*-shame, moreover, suggests that it might be a terrible mistake to identify the Chinese ethical viewpoint as being based on a shame culture as many scholars have assumed in their response to Benedict's theory of Asian cultures. Of course, given that it is based on her anthropological investigation into to what she saw as the "Japanese culture," my analysis of the Chinese concept of *chi*-shame here is relevant to her viewpoint insofar as we recognize the close affiliation between the concept of *chi* in Chinese and the concept of *haji* in Japanese. It is important to note here that my study only aims at clarifying the content of *chi*-shame in the context of classical Chinese philosophy and showing how the field of Sinology must reconsider the conventional distinction of shame and guilt that it has imported from the Anglo-European perspectives on ethics.

Given that the concept of *chi*-shame is not the same as the English concept of shame, and also that *chi* is neither shame nor guilt in their distinct separation from each other, I will clarify in the following both common features and major differences between *chi* and shame by conducting a comparative study of them. Then, I will turn to a historical study of the classical Chinese texts and point out two major issues: (1) according to Mencius's designation of "the heart of *xiu*-shame and disdain (*xiuwu-zhixin* 羞惡之心)," the meaning of *chi*-shame is traditionally understood as an internal, self-reflective experience that we can characterize as the ethical; and (2) in line with Wang Chuanshan's (王船山, 1619–1692) commentary on Mencius's concept of "cultivation of *qi*" (*yangqi* 养气) in *Mengzi* 2A2, I argue that the function of *chi* is to lead an agent to self-examination and ultimately to build up its moral courage.[10] Far from being a reactionary embarrassment that has nothing to do with an internal process of ethical reflection, the Chinese notion of *chi* suggests a complex emotional, moral response that a person has towards its own self or others over a certain state of affairs.

A Comparative Study of Shame in the Anglo-European Context

This comparative study of the notion of "shame" aims at exploring the content of *chi*-shame, which is particularly rooted in the history of Chinese philosophy. My intention here, therefore, is not to evaluate the concept of shame or guilt as they are understood in the development of morality or ethics in the Anglo-European philosophical context but to answer the following questions: What would it be like to have a concept that unites both shame and guilt (as they are often separated from each other in dominant theories of ethics in contemporary Anglo-European philosophy)? What are the necessary implications of having this concept in the theory of ethics? To provide readers with a basic framework for understanding the distinct characteristics of *chi*, I would like to refer to Martha Nussbaum's and Bernard Williams's renderings of "shame" and "guilt" as a foil and use it for elucidating the Chinese concept of *chi*.

Williams grounds his interpretation of shame on Homer's classical poetry and argues that shame and guilt were not obviously distinct from each other in the ancient Greek world. Then, he explains how shame can be associated with guilt to the extent where they can forge an ethical identity in a realistic fashion. At the outset, it may seem that *chi*-shame would be identical with the ancient Greek concept of shame (αιδως or αισχύνη). However, Williams further qualifies his argument by saying that the Greek concept does not share all the

---

10   I rely on Wang Chuanshan's commentary for making my claim in this chapter
     because he specifically demonstrated the content of the "cultivation of *qi*" with the
     function of *chi*-shame. As he claims, "the cultivation of *qi* is mutually embodied
     and applied with the heart of *xiu*-shame and disdain to the most extent." Fuzhi
     Wang, *Discourse on Reading the Great Collection of Commentaries on the Four Books*
     (Beijing: Zhonghua Shuju, 1975), 539.

implications of guilt because the sense of shame in general is neutral and not necessarily related to morality.[11] At the end of the analysis, he cannot deny that shame is irreducible to guilt or that they are quite different from each other. Williams's theory still holds that shame is a primitive experience or an immediate reaction to the state of being seen: hence, the experience of shame can push an agent in two directions: (1) it can make her hide herself (and this would be a negative response to the experience of shame) or (2) it moves her to improve her behavior (and this would be a positive reconstitution of her character.) Either way, Williams argues, the ashamed agent is simply looking at her own self-image. The experience of guilt, however, must be evoked by other's anger towards self: hence, it can only lead the self to look for the possibility of making amends with the victim of her action.[12]

The problem of this distinction between shame and guilt is that the victim's anger does not immediately incite the feeling of guilt in the agent, since she needs to become aware of why and how her action have harmed the victim and led to the other's negative emotion towards itself. One may argue that the self can also feel guilty simply by violating a certain rule or principle. In this case, she does not have to recognize the victim's anger. However, Williams dismisses this type of self-imposed guilt as being irrational because it can ignore the important moral factors as agent's voluntariness, the consequence of her act, and her relation to the victim.[13] Williams in this sense argues that (reasonable) guilt should be associated with shame in order to have a realistic picture of moral life. Since shame looks at the agent's self-image, it embodies self-reflective attentiveness to her inter-relation with others. Thus, the concept of shame can help us make sense of our act that victimizes the other or understand the appropriate amends that we would have to make with the other for an ethical reconciliation.[14]

The interrelation of shame and guilt in Williams's account shares many features with the notion of *chi*-shame in the classical Chinese

---

11   Williams, *Shame and Necessity*, 92.
12   Williams, 88–92.
13   Williams, 93.
14   Williams, 94.

philosophy. By this statement, I simply mean that self's responsibility is measured in light of her assessment of self-image. The term, *chi*, exactly functions in the same way. Nevertheless, it would be quite misleading to think that Williams's model is identical with a traditional understanding of *chi*-shame. That is because Williams's notion of shame is not yet a single unified emotion with guilt. It is unclear how his rendering of guilt can complement shame in his account. Nor does he clearly show the ground in which shame can make a person respond to a single state of affairs (that is to be seen by the other) in two diametrically opposed ways. Contrariwise, the concept of *chi* carries the necessary implications of both shame and guilt; and because of that, it carries a new function that is inexplicable by either one of these terms: namely the function of cultivating agent's emotional and intellectual confidence in being morally responsible. This distinct character of *chi*-shame, which cannot be found in Williams's account of shame in reference to ancient Greek philosophy, can be found in *Mengzi* 2A2. I will revisit this point later in this chapter.

We cannot show how *chi*-shame in classical Chinese philosophy is more comprehensive than the Ancient Greek version of αιδώς or αισχύνη by looking at Williams's account of shame and guilt alone. It is helpful here to consult Nussbaum's psychoanalysis. *Pace* Williams, Nussbaum recognizes that one's primordial experience of guilt is evoked by someone else's anger; but what is different from Williams's account is that she applies a method of psychoanalysis for identifying the negative aspect of shame, which leads us to a conclusion that the self-image, embodied by the experience of shame, can be narcissistic.[15] Her analysis begins with an investigation into infancy. When we look at a baby, it is self-evident that she needs to rely on her caretakers for her provisions and her perception of the world, as well as her own self, are determined by her relationship with these caring others. Should these caretakers neglect to meet her needs, the baby, left alone to her own self, would have to feel helpless in her own world. However, when her needs are met by these caretakers, she would feel omnipotent and utterly optimistic about her world. When the infant

---

15   Martha C Nussbaum, *Hiding from Humanity: Disgust, Shame, and the Law* (Princeton and Oxford: Princeton University Press., 2004), 207.

cultivates an awareness that the caretakers are a distinct being that she cannot control, she comes to recognize the distance between her real- and ideal-self. Nussbaum argues that the sense of shame emerges out of this awareness;[16] and echoes Aristophanes' portrait of shame in Plato's *Symposium*: "a painful emotion grounded in the recognition of our own non-omnipotence and lack of control."[17]

Nussbaum shows that, on the one hand, shame can be negative especially when it fails to give the sense of omnipotence to a person feeling it. In this case, the person in shame can feel like hiding her real, vulnerable self behind a robotic and inauthentic "false self."[18] On the other hand, the sense of shame can be positive if it guides the person to admit that she is incomplete and powerless by herself, thereby recognizing the rights of others and learning to reciprocate her goods with others.[19] The sense of guilt is much more elaborate and comprehensive than this image of shame. Guilt, Nussbaum argues, originates when a child becomes aware of her aggressive desire to harm another human being. In order for this to happen, the child must be aware that her caretakers have their own rights prior to experiencing the sense of guilt. This clearly suggests that guilt aims at making amends with other for the sake of the other and thereby much more explicitly avoids failing victim to the problem of narcissism.[20]

So how does Nussbaum talk about the relation of shame and guilt? I must say that her account is flawless. When these two terms are tied together in an agent, she is capable of measuring the distance between her real- and ideal self, thereby clearly seeing how much harm she has done to others. This moral self-reflection suggests a conversion: the person turns away from the self-centeredness of only caring for her own self-image to an other-centered perspective where she can weigh the negative impact of her self-affirmative act or desire on others around her. In this sense, the narcissistic quality of shame will be peeled away as it tied to the sense of guilt. Furthermore, the integration of shame and guilt in the person requires her to be emotionally

---

16   Nussbaum, 197–99.
17   Nussbaum, 182.
18   Nussbaum, 192.
19   Nussbaum, 188.
20   Nussbaum, 207.

mature and ethically intelligent. She will exhibit her willingness to be moral (whether or not she is aware of this fact in herself). Otherwise, Nussbaum seems to argue, the agent will not be able to compare and examine her self-image with her responsibility to others. Nor will she know why her (real or ideal) self-image has an impact on her connection with others in human society.[21]

According to Williams, the association of shame and guilt affords a moral self a distinct character. The self can arrive at a moral principle through an assessment of her self-image and because of that, she can consider how to realize the moral principle in relativity to her life circumstances. In Williams's account, shame is not only distinct from guilt but seems to serve as a practical anchor for realizing one's moral ideal and further as a necessary condition for the possibility of feeling guilty since this is felt when measuring one's deviation from the ideal-self. Simply put, a guilt without the shame tends to be unrealistic. Nussbaum also recognizes a distinction and interrelation between shame and guilt like Williams. However, Nussbaum suggests that there could be a hierarchical relation in which guilt is emotionally and psychologically more comprehensive than shame. Stated succinctly, a shame without the guilt tends to be immature.

My argument is that *chi* is even more progressive than Nussbaum's and Williams's account of shame and guilt. The concept of *chi*-shame combines shame and guilt altogether while they simply argue how they are related. In other words, a challenged self-image (i.e., shame) and the feeling of responsibility (i.e., guilt) are integral moments of the notion of "being ashamed" in the sense of *chi* in Chinese. In the following, I would like to demonstrate this point in four steps: First, I will explain the connection between one's assessment of self-image (as shame) and awareness of moral responsibility (as guilt) in *chi*-shame. Second, I will show how *chi* leads an agent to have a more realistic understanding of her moral life in relativity to particular and historical circumstances in

---

21   The "harm" can refer to an agent's action, whether it has been or has not been done to another; the former case signifies an actual wrongdoing, but the latter case signifies the inadequate realization of a duty or responsibility. For instance, a father's physical abuse is definitely a kind of harm to his child; but on the other hand, even though the father did nothing abusive, his irresponsible negligence can be recognized as a kind of harm to his child, too.

which she is situated. Third, the self-image embodied in *chi*-shame is formed in relation to the other rather than self. Fourth, self in response to *chi*-shame makes an effort to fulfill her responsibility such that she can further develop, and even preserve if necessary, her self-image without falling victim to the problem of narcissistic self-centrism.

A Hermenuetics of Classical Chinese Texts

My representation of the notion of *chi* as shame in Chinese culture is based on an interpretation of the term in the classical Confucian tradition. More specifically, I am referring to the *Mengzi* 2A2. This is far from advocating any innovative reading of the famous text. However, because the earlier investigations of the concept of shame in the field of Sinology and Chinese philosophy have failed to pay due attention to the distinction between *xiu* and *chi*, my take on the notion of shame in Chinese philosophy here may sound quite controversial to many scholars. I am also aware that it is incredibly awkward to use the term "shame" to describe *chi* (especially when we simply read the texts in Chinese). Nevertheless, precisely because the prior assumption that Chinese culture is a "shame culture" and also because most Anglophone publications on the notion of "shame" in the Chinese classical tradition have used this term to translate *xiu* and *chi* interchangeably, I am using the term "*chi*-shame" to break away from the terrible equivocation in translation. At the end of this chapter, it should become clear to readers that *chi* is best described as "shame-guilt" if we respect the distinction of these concepts that abovementioned philosophers as Nussbaum and Williams have made in reference to ancient Greek philosophy.

In the following, I would like to indicate three points while keeping this distinction between shame and guilt:

1. *Chi*-shame is both internal and ethical.
2. *Chi*-shame is equivalent to Mencius's designation of the "heart of *xiu*-shame and disdain."
3. *Chi*-shame is always already inclusive of guilt.

When these points are taken together, we will be able to see that a proper understanding of *chi*-shame indicates an inseparability of shame and guilt (as these terms are understood in the field of European ethics) and the term, *chi*, should not be equivocated either with shame or guilt but understood as the unity of both terms.

Different Meaning of Chi

Brian Van Norden draws a stark division between internal and external shame when he talks about two paradigms of it in English. On the one hand, there is a "conventional shame," which indicates "a sort of unpleasant feeling we have when we believe those whose views matter to us look down on us, on the basis of a standard of appearance we share."[22] On the other hand, there is an "ethical shame," which points to "a sort of unpleasant feeling we have when we believe that we have significant character flaws."[23] The former is external in the sense that the cause of the displeasure comes from outside self while the latter is internal since it requires a self-reflection vis-à-vis one's ethical character. If we borrow Van Norden's distinction, *chi* would have to be an internal/ethical shame; whereas *xiu* is inclusive of (but not limited to) the external/conventional shame. The conventional/external shame as *xiu*-shame can be found everywhere in *Xunzi*. Most of these examples refer to a violation of rites or a display of bad social manners.[24] The internal/ethical shame, on the other, shows up as a perplexing passage in the *Analects* 8.13:

邦有道，貧且賤焉，恥也；邦無道，富且貴焉，恥也。

When a country is well-governed, poverty and a mean condition are things to be ashamed of. When a country is ill-governed, riches and honor are things to be ashamed of.[25]

---

22   Norden, "The Emotion of Shame and the Virtue of Righteousness in Mencius," 60.

23   Norden, 61.

24   Through the examples of *xiu*-shame, Jane Geaney concludes that the Chinese concept of shame is structured in a "contact-driven" and "boundary-blurring" metaphor, it is different from the "sexual/visible" metaphor in the English concept. See Geaney, "Moral Boundaries: Shame in Early Confucianism."

25   James Legge, "Tai Bo," in *Chinese Text Project*, n.d., https://ctext.org/analects/tai-bo/ens.

At the outset, this sentence seems to be saying that external goods are the cause of internal/ethical shame. Confucius does not deny this, as what he has stated in the first sentence. However, a closer look at the passage clearly shows that neither poverty nor wealth by itself can be the cause of *chi*-shame; instead, it is caused by an agent's failure to fulfill her responsibility to uphold peace and economic balance in each society. What we see here is that an educated person in the Confucian context is obliged to engage in the civil service and make a contribution to her society. If she succeeds, the rewards will satisfy her material needs. Accordingly, she must be *chi*-ashamed of her poverty, because she has failed to gain a position in a well-governed country since this can mean either that she lacks her ability to fulfill the duty or is unwilling to do so. By the same token, she should be *chi*-ashamed of her riches when she gains a government position in an ill-governed country. This can mean that she has failed to execute good governance for the people or that she has abused her position with a series of corruptions. In both passages, we can see that *chi*-shame both in poverty and wealth is tied to one's failure in civic and moral responsibility. It clearly implicates a sense of guilt in the ashamed agent.

Confucius also refuses a view that a poor appearance would be chi-shameful when it is not caused by irresponsibility.[26] The *Analects* 4.9, for instance argues:

士志於道，而恥惡衣惡食者，未足與議也。

A scholar, whose mind is set on truth, and who is ashamed of bad clothes and bad food, is not fit to be discoursed with.[27]

This passage shows that one can be *chi*-ashamed of one's poor appearance, and this is ethically undesirable. The sense of shame as *chi*, in other words, can transcend what is considered to be appropriate in terms of social etiquette. In reference to the same passage, Heiner

---

26   Bongrae Seok refuses to make a distinction between external or internal to identify *chi*-shame; he concludes that *chi*-shame is "one's self-reflective concern for a personal integrity and a good life in a community...." See Seok, "Moral Psychology of Shame in Early Confucian Philosophy," 125, 132.

27   James Legge, "Li Ren," in *Chinese Text Project*, n.d., https://ctext.org/analects/li-ren/ens.

Roetz even goes so far as to say that shame in the Chinese concept is "no less efficient for a post-conventional morality than the inner experience of guilt."[28] I concur with Roetz's conclusion here and his statement certainly supports my argument. But I would add another qualification to his statement by saying that *chi*-shame is not simply analogous to guilt but contains it. This point may not be explicit to many contemporary interpreters of the *Analects*. However, Mencius's interpretation of righteousness certainly supports Roetz's and my reading.

Mencius defines four cardinal moral attributes in *Mengzi* 2A6: (1) benevolence 仁, (2) propriety 禮, (3) wisdom 智, and (4) righteousness 義. He argues that the fourth and the last virtue, righteousness, grows from the "heart of *xiu*-shame and disdain." Zhu Xi in his commentary on Mencius's expression further argues that

羞，恥己之不善也。惡，憎人之不善也。

Xiu-shame is to be *chi*-ashamed about what is not good in oneself. Disdain is to hate what is not good in others"[29]

Van Norden supplements Zhu Xi's commentary by saying that the emotion of disdain must be understood in terms of the function of shame, as the reason of the emotion of disdain does not necessarily suggest that the agent is aware of her character flaw: hence, it is not sufficient to signify the virtue of righteousness.[30] The flipside of this argument is that Mencius' concept of "heart of *xiu*-shame and disdain," which grows the virtue of righteousness, is based on self-image, namely shame (*xiu* 羞) as it is generally understood in English. I further argue that the concept of responsibility, namely guilt, must be included here in the definition of *chi*-shame as the unity of *xiu* and *è* (disdain in original) too: hence, Mencius' notion of "heart of *xiu*-shame and disdain" is equivalent to the concept of *chi*-shame.

---

28   Roetz, *Confucian Ethics of the Axial Age*, 181.

29   Xi Zhu, *Collected Commentaries on the Four Books (Sishu Zhangju Jizhu)* (Beijing: Zhonghua Shuju, 1983), 237.

30   Van Norden, "The Emotion of Shame and the Virtue of Righteousness in Mencius," 66.

Zhu Xi's commentary renders the distinction of *xiu* and disdain to the direction they are facing (inward or outward), and explains that *xiu*-shame means being "ashamed" of own's fault in the sense of *chi*, and the term "disdain," means to hate other's fault. Interestingly, it also makes sense to say in Chinese that "I am *chi*-ashamed of other's fault," which suggests that "*chi*" and "disdain" can also be used interchangeably. For instance, *Mengzi* 1B3 says:

一人衡行于天下，武王恥之。此武王之勇也。而武王亦一怒而安天下之民。

There was one who behaved obstinately in the world, and King Wu was (*chi*-) ashamed of this. This was the valor of King Wu. So, King Wu, too, brought peace to all the people in the world with one burst of anger.

Mencius is clearly saying that King Wu is praiseworthy for his valor where he would be "(*chi*-)ashamed" of the others' fault instead of his own. This shows that the sense of shame in Chinese *chi* must include the concept of responsibility to some extent. Van Norden has acknowledged this point in his reading of this passage when he says that *chi*-shame must be similar to guilt as it also evokes righteous anger in the context of classical Chinese. However, we can easily detect his hesitation towards the equation of *chi*-shame and guilt when he concludes his observation with the following statement: "Confucian shame is not like guilt in anticipating the righteous anger of others; insofar as righteous rage is connected with shame, it is anger toward oneself, or toward others who subject oneself to shame."[31]

My argument here is simply to point out the validity of Van Norden's insight: that is to say, *chi*-shame contains guilt. King Wu's shame towards others' fault is deriving from the fact that he feels responsible for others' actions as this state of affairs took place under his rule. King Wu's feeling of shame is clearly elicited by his self-assessment of responsibility, that is much more than reflecting on his self-image; and further the passage shows with an image of righteous anger where *Wu-wang* is definitely suffering from the sense of guilt towards himself at the same time. If this reading is possible (as I believe it is), we have to say that King Wu's *chi*-shame in Mencius' reading of it (in

---

31   Van Norden, 70.

consonance with Xu Zhi's interpretation) represents a combination of shame (*xiu*) and guilt. Recall Williams' and Nussbaum's accounts. If these two senses of shame and guilt were not implicit in the notion of *chi*-shame, *Wu-wang's* emotion of shame over others' fault seems to be either childish or irrational. If it were not associated with the feeling of guilt while containing his self-assessment of responsibility as a ruler, Nussbaum's observation becomes relevant: his feeling of shame would have to be based on a childish illusion that he is the omnipotent owner of the world as *his* world. If the feeling of *chi*-shame had nothing to do with the emotion of *xiu*, regardless of the fact that it is derived from his self-image as the ruler of the kingdom, his feeling of guilt over others' actions, as Williams has rightly portrayed, would have to look quite irrational.

The Function of Chi-*Shame*

The term, "*chi*," does not appear in *Mengzi* 2A2. Yet my reading of it is in line with Chuanshan's commentary. Chuanshan (also known as Wang Fuzhi 王夫之, 1619–1692) is recognized as the greatest Chinese philosopher after Wang Yangming (王陽明, 1472–1529). His theory of moral cultivation set forth the idea that "to know to be shameful is akin to courage" (*zhichi jinhu yong* 知恥近乎勇),[32] which originates from Confucius's expression in *The Doctrine of the Mean*.[33] Chuanshan states that *Mengzi* 2A2 has revealed the function of the "heart of shame and disdain,"[34] which I have shown above as the equivalent to *chi*-shame. This is to say that my reading of the section 2A2 is consistent with Wang Fuzhi's commentary on the same pas-

---

32   Wing-Tsit Chan's translation, see Wing-Tsit Chan, *A Source Book In Chinese Philosophy* (New Jersey: Princeton University Press, 1963), 105.

33   This is noted by Tang Junyi, see Junyi Tang, "On Education (Yuan-Jiao-Pian)," *Fundamental Exposition of Chinese Philosophy* (Zhong-Guo-Zhe-Xue-Yuan-Lun) (Beijing: Zhonghua Shehui Kexue Chubanshe, 2006), 393. Chuanshan is relatively unknown in English studies of Chinese philosophy, for more information on him, see JeeLoo Liu's introduction: "Wang Fuzhi (Wang Fu-Chich)," in *Encyclopedia of Chinese Philosophy*, ed. Antonis S. Cua (New York: Rouledge, 2003), 748–55.

34   Wang, *Discourse on Reading the Great Collection of Commentaries on the Four Books*, 539.

sage. This interpretation may sound questionable to many scholars of classical Chinese philosophy in Anglo-European academia. That is precisely because the prior translations of the passage, including the versions made by Irene Bloom, Van Norden, Jane Rainey, and James Legge, cannot satisfactorily convey the meaning of what they have translated as "shame." At the same time they significantly diverge from each other regarding their translations of the relevant expressions.[35] (Perhaps that is because they seem to have very different ideas about how to make the Chinese expressions comprehensible in English.) Having said that, I believe I can substantiate my reading of the passage in light of Chuanshan's commentary. I will do this by taking the following three steps: first, I will quote the most literal translation of the passages in question; second, I will indicate the problems that arise from reading it; and finally, I will refer to Wang Fuzhi's commentary for dissolving the issues.

Mengzi 2A2 starts with Mencius's disciple, Gongshun Chou's (公孫丑) question: Will his mind be moved if he is appointed as the prime minister? Mencius replies to this question by saying that he has attained an "unmoved mind" (*bu-dong-xin* 不動心) since the age of forty. Chou then begs Mencius to elaborate on the method of cultivating this great mind. Mencius initially claims that it is equivalent to the "nourishment of courage" (*yang-yong* 養勇) and with some examples, argues that the most praiseworthy method for attaining this virtue is to engage in a kind of moral self-examination.

Gongshun Chou further begs Mencius to compare his virtue of unmoved mind with Gaozi's (告子) notion of it. The teacher continues his instruction with a claim that he has surpassed Gaozi's state of *budongxin* because his great mind implies two other virtues, such as "understanding words," (*zhiyan* 知言) and "good at nourishing my flood-like vital-force (*shanyang wu haoranzhiqi* 善養吾浩然之氣)." The arguments end with an illustration of what these virtues are. The point of my interpretation in this section is that Mencius's expressions

---

35   Irene Bloom, *Mencius*, ed. Philip J. Ivanhoe (New York: Columbia University Press, 2009); Bryan W. Van Norden, *Readings in Classical Chinese Philosophy*, ed. Philip J. Ivanhoe (New York: Seven Bridge Press, 2001); Lee Rainey, "Mencius and His Vast, Overflowing Qi (Hao ran zhi qi)," *Monumenta Serica*, no. 46 (1998): 92.

as "nourishment of vital-force" (養氣) and "nourishment of courage" (養勇) basically refer to the function of *chi*-shame.

The questions and answers raised in the 2A2 seem incomprehensible to many readers (especially in English) because the notion of "vital-force," or more precisely, the translation of the famous term, *qi* (氣), is quite confusing for contemporary readers. *Qi* in ancient Chinese signifies the fundamental essence of the universe, and it can be understood as either the matter or energy of everything, or the whole cosmos. The term, *yangqi*, can basically refer to anything whatsoever. This polyvocal nature of the critical term makes the 2A2 quite perplexing precisely because the objects that the vital-force refers to can vary from one sentence to another. In this sense, it is important to set the baseline of our reading. My method is to trace back Mencius's narrative: that is to say, I will first clarify what he means by "nourishment of vital-force," secondly elucidates its implication in relation to the "nourishment of courage," and lastly outlines the significance of the "unmoved mind."[36]

The discourse on *yangqi* consists of three parts. The first part explains the major characteristics of the vital-force; the second illustrates how one should nourish it in oneself; the last presents the caveat where Mencius warns that one should not force its growth. The first part reads:

> 其爲氣也，至大至剛，以直養而無害，則塞于天地之閒。其爲氣也，配義與道；無是，餒也。

> This vital-force is exceedingly great and exceedingly strong. If one nourishes it with uprightness and does not harm it, it will fill up all between heaven and earth. This vital-force associates the righteousness and the way [the universal doctrine]. Without these, it starves.

It is clear that *yang-qi* refers to something that is equipped with a moral quality, and also that it needs to be extended by an agent. The question is whether it signifies the movement of the universe or the development of an individual's capacity. Rainey recognizes this

---

36   I skip the discourse about "understanding words," since it is not nearly so relevant to Chi-shame; it signifies the tranquil mind that prevents the agent from being affected by harmful speech.

ambivalence when she argues that it can be both. Since the "right-eousness" is inherent in both the universe and humanity, the agent's extension of vital-force must mean that by the restoration of her inherent righteousness, she can unite herself with the movement of the universe.[37] We can see that Rainey's interpretation of the first part requires a cosmological viewpoint where the universe and humans are inherently correlated (if not entirely fused) with each other. I hesitate to fully embrace Rainey's viewpoint for a historical reason. This type of a cosmological argument was not available till the emergence of the Yin-Yang School in 325–240 BCE, which would be antecedent to Mencius' death at least by several decades.

Then, how can we explain Mencius' expression that the vital-force "will fill up all that is between heaven and earth" without resorting to the cosmological interpretation? Chuanshan's commentary can help us make sense of this passage. In his *Discourse on Reading the Great Collection of Commentaries on the Four Books* (讀四書大全說) he argues that it would be absurd to understand this expression in the physical sense. Hence, he suggests to read this statement as saying that a person is potentially capable of making all things in the world righteous through her moral effort because nothing external to her can obstruct her willingness to act righteously.[38] This interpretation is in consonance with Mencius's other line in 7A4: "All things are complete in us" (萬物皆備於我矣). In light of this passage, he argues that the word "complete" (備) must be understood as signifying one's potentiality. The first part thus shows that the vital-force refers to an individual's capacity of doing what is righteous (義); and its extension to heaven and earth indicates a projection of her righteousness onto the surrounding world (rather implicating a correspondence of the universe and the subject in the cosmological argument). The first section, thus, implies two inter-related theoretical points that nothing can prevent a human being from projecting her view of *yi* to everything and also that everything can be

---

37   Rainey, 'Mencius and His Vast, Overflowing Qi (HAO RAN ZHI QI)', 103.

38   Wang, *Discourse on Reading the Great Collection of Commentaries on the Four Books*, 536–37; Fuzhi Wang, *A Contemporary Interpretation of the Meaning of the Four Books*, vol. 8, Collection of Chuanshan's Works (Chuan-Shan-Quan-Shu) (Hu Nan: Yuelu Shushe, 1988), 191.

reached by her capacity to embody righteousness. The second part of the 2A2 reads as the following:

是集義所生者，非義襲而取之也。行有不慊於心，則餒矣。我故曰，告子未嘗知義，以其外之也。

The vital-force (i.e., the capacity of doing righteousness) is produced by the accumulation of righteousness. It cannot be obtained by a seizure of righteousness. If the mind does not feel complacency in conduct, the vital-force becomes starved. I therefore said, Gaozi has never understood righteousness, because he makes it something external.

We can verify two things from this passage. First, Mencius's idea of righteousness is internal to a subject. This is quite different from Gaozi's view. Second, one's "capacity to do what is righteousness," which is what Mencius must mean by the term "vital-force," can be undermined by one's mind. This point is conveyed by the image in which a mind can be deprived of *qi* to its starvation. Mencius's expression does not explicitly tell us what kind of emotion is related to the state where "the mind does not feel complacency in conduct." Moreover, it is unclear what he means by the phrase, "seizure of righteousness" (*yi-xi* 義襲), and why it has to be placed in an opposition to the "accumulation of righteousness"(*ji-yi* 集義) in the same sentence.

The "seizure of righteousness" comes from Van Norden's literal translation of *yixi*. The others, including Legge, Bloom, and Rainey paraphrase it with different terms as the "sporadic-" or "occasional-show of righteousness." These paraphrases indeed highlight the contrast between *yixi* and *jiyi*; and yet fail to explain why Mencius had to use the metaphorical language of "seizure." Chinese semantics makes it clear that Mencius's phrase is implicitly saying that righteousness is not a foreign object that we can capture from someone or somewhere else, and this point is also consistent with his later criticism of Gaozi.

Chuanshan's commentary remains attentive to all of these ambiguities and gives a definitive reading of the passage. He argues that the content of righteousness can always change depending on different circumstances.[39] This is to say that an act, which has been widely rec-

---

39   Wang, *Discourse on Reading the Great Collection of Commentaries on the Four Books*, 534.

ognized as a righteous behavior for years in a society could be perni-
cious and far from being morally upright when it is absolutized without paying due attention to the concrete context in which it is to be
carried out. Stated succinctly, when the action results from a careless
formality, an act of righteousness could be devoid of content, thus
failing to be righteous at the end.[40] The language of "seizure" refers
to a dogmatic imitation of a moral act which carelessly grabs the
formal appearance of righteousness but ends up filling itself with a
false value. In this sense, the expression *yixi* diametrically opposes the
phrase "accumulation of righteousness," and what Mencius is saying
here is that any form of righteousness must accompany one's moral
self-examination as its content.

Wang Fuzhi further claims that Mencius's expression, "the mind
does not feel complacency in conduct," indicates a long-term result
of the "accumulation of righteousness" rather than pointing at a random moment in which a (seemingly) righteous act is repeatedly carried out. He draws our attention to Mencius's earlier insight that the
"heart of shame and disdain grow righteousness," as he points out
here that the state in which "the mind does not feel complacency
in conduct" signifies a disappearance of shame (*chi*) after a rigorous
moral self-examination. The emotion of *chi*, in other words, moves
a person to engage in an endless process of self-critique where she
will continuously question how she can be righteous at all. Without
recognizing the importance of a continuous self-betterment at the
beginning of this *jiyi*, she will suffer from her delusional confidence in
her self-righteousness. In this case, the "seizure of righteousness" will
forever keep her capacity to become a morally upright person, namely
yangqi, from realizing its full potentiality.[41] This is exactly what Mencius means by the image of how "vital-force becomes starved" ((氣)
則餒也). The capacity to do what is right, according to *Mengzi* 2A2,
requires our "confidence in being righteous," whose development, in
turn, calls for a series of self-examinations motivated by *chi*-shame.

---

40   Wang, *A Contemporary Interpretation of the Meaning of the Four Books*, 8:192.
41   Wang, *Discourse on Reading the Great Collection of Commentaries on the Four
        Books*, 538–40; Wang, *A Contemporary Interpretation of the Meaning of the Four
        Books*, 8:192.

The central of role of *chi*-shame as the initiator of self-examination, which is requisite for realizing one's moral righteousness, becomes far more explicit in the third and concluding part:

必有事焉而勿正，心勿忘，勿助長也。

Always be doing something, but without fixation. Let the heart not forget, but do not help it grow.

The term "without fixation" is Bloom's literal translation of *wu-zheng* (勿正) while the other versions use different phrases that do not necessarily share the same meaning.[42] Zhu Xi's commentary makes it clear that it should mean "without expectation" (正，預期也).[43] The Anglophone translators have opted for different terms probably because the expression "without expectation" sounds as though we are insinuating a maxim that a person should not deliberately initiate the process of her "accumulation of righteousness." This also leaves us with a further conundrum: what does Mencius mean by the phrase "we should not help (*qi* 氣) grow"?

Zhu Xi's interpretation can help us make sense of this passage once we recognize his point that a nourishment of vital-force, namely cultivating our capacity to do what is of righteousness, essentially signifies the growth of our confidence in doing so. Given that the growth of confidence is the result of self-examination instigated by *chi*, one's expectation of it will remove her feeling of *chi*-shame in her act of righteousness. Since *chi* contains the sense of guilt, this sense of shame implies an assessment of self's responsibility and self-image. In this case, our experience of shame should make us realize that our dogmatic expectation of the growth of *qi* is both vain and delusional. That is to say, the "growth of confidence" (namely *zhangqi*

---

42   Rainey translates it as "no stop", see Rainey, "Mencius and His Vast, Overflowing Qi (Hao ran zhi qi)," 91. Van Norden renders it as "do not aim at it directly," see Van Norden, *Readings in Classical Chinese Philosophy*, 123. While Legge terms it as "without the object of thereby nourishing the passion-nature." See James Legge, trans., "Gong Sun Chou I," in *Chinese Text Project*, n.d., https://ctext.org/mengzi/gong-sun-chou-i/ens. As you can see, they widely differ from each other and I do not think these readings are accurately capturing what Mencius is saying here.

43   Zhu, *Sishu zhangju jizhu*, 232.

長氣) should be the natural outcome of the "accumulation of right-eousness." It is simply hypocritical if a person expects it to automatically grow on its own. Instead, she must always be humble and never forget to question herself if she can possibly be confident in her being a righteous person. Chuanshan demonstrates that those who rigidly abide by a certain regiment or routine without reflecting on the general principles that substantiate its meaning or mindlessly disdain vices without thinking about the reasons why they should be hated, are hollow pretenders. They act as though they are contributing to the growth of vital-force but are in fact far from growing their capacity to embody what the idea, 義 *yi*, signifies.[44]

Thus, the content of the "nourishment of vital-force" (養氣) is equivalent to the "nourishment of courage," and both are requisite for attaining an authentic, moral confidence. This authentic confidence, however, cannot be delusional self-confidence where a self simply assumes its capacity to grow *qi* and uncritically expects its destiny to eventually embody morally perfection. Rather, it must be a paradoxical confidence where the self always recognizes the necessity of self-examination and with continuous and profound humility, it always finds a room for self-betterment. This selfless confidence in an authentic self-image is in fact what Mencius means by the term, "unmoved mind" (*budongxin* 不動心).

Mencius explicitly states in Chinese that the most praiseworthy way to nourish one's courage for attaining the *budongxin* is through *zifan* (自反), namely self-examination:

自反而不縮，雖褐寬博，吾不惴焉；自反而縮，雖千萬人，吾往矣。

If, on looking inward, I find that I am not upright, I must be in fear of even a poor fellow in coarse clothing. If, on looking inward, I find that I am upright, I may proceed against thousands and tens of thousands.[45]

The term "in fear" (*suo* 縮) however, seems quite incompatible with the general understanding of what we mean by "courage" or

---

44 Wang, *A Contemporary Interpretation of the Meaning of the Four Books*, 8:193; Wang, *Discourse on Reading the Great Collection of Commentaries on the Four Books*, 534.

45 Bloom, *Mencius*, 49.

"unmoved mind" in English. Van Norden defines the "*budongxin*" as meaning "to fail to be disturbed or frightened."[46] With this understanding of the term, he indicates that there are two possible interpretations: (1) "It [*suo*] may mean that true courage requires being afraid if one finds that one is in the wrong." Or, (2) "being afraid when one recognizes that one is not upright is not part of 'great courage'; rather, 'great courage' consists only in 'going forward' when one recognizes that one is upright."[47] Simply put, a person is in fear when she realizes that she is not upright. But then how could this be consonant with her quality of being fearless since that seems to be what Mencius (*à la* Van Norden) means by her "unmoved mind"(which is fearless)?

Van Norden embraces both interpretations in terms of the person's feeling of fear is not directed at the loss of her well-being, but of another's loss. He states:

> [Those who are fully virtuous] do not feel fear when righteousness requires them to sacrifice their lives. In addition, the fully courageous may be frightened by the prospect of the suffering of others and may be saddened by the absence of things like familial love. However, even when perturbed in these ways, the fully courageous continue to manifest motivational harmony.[48]

That means, for Van Norden, that a person's mind could have been moved due to her feeling of fear, but her fear leads her to have "true courage" as long as (1) her fear is caused by the fact that she is concerned with whether or not she has done some harm to the other or (2) her fear manifests her "great courage" where she continues to give her help to others because her fear indicates her concerns with the well-being of the other. In either case, Van Norden shows that her commitment to being upright is unmoved, thus reaching the "motivational harmony" regardless of the fact that she is experiencing the emotion of "fear."

My interpretation of 2A2 is consistent with Van Norden's reading here. One's negative emotion, such as fear, over against one's failure

---

46   Bryan W. Van Norden, "Mencius on Courage," *Midwest Studies in Philosophy*, 21 (1997): 240.
47   Van Norden, 247.
48   Van Norden, 249–50.

to be righteous is triggered by another's failure. This suggests that the negative emotion must be evoked to some extent by the sense of responsibility. However, I disagree with his reading of the "unmoved mind" as the strength of one's moral will. I argue, *pace* Wang Fuzhi, that it represents a moral confidence. This is clear from the fact that Mencius immediately cancels his praise of Gaozi's *budongxin* by making a serious critique: "Gaozi never understood what is *yi* (義) since he had regarded it as something external to one's existence." Mencius's understanding of the "unmoved mind" does not rely on the presence of moral willingness in a person (as Van Norden's interpretation indicates) but the presence of moral knowledge, where an authentic self engages in an endless process of self-examination, thereby achieving her accumulation of righteousness both with profound humility and exuberant vital-force.

The chapter, *Gongsun Chou* 公孫丑, part one (namely the overture to the 2A2), shows a student asking his teacher: "Will his mind be moved if he becomes the prime minister?" Zhu Xi's commentary rephrases the question:

任大責重如此，亦有所恐懼疑惑而動其心乎？

With such great responsibility, will you be afraid, be in doubt, of having your mind moved?[49]

Zhu Xi's reading shows that both "courage" and "unmoved mind" must refer to the "confidence in being responsible." This explains why "self-examination" (自反) is noted by Mencius as the most praiseworthy way to nourish courage, because, once again without it, one's confidence or courage might turn out to be delusional and groundless. By the same token, the presence of fear does not conflict with the virtue of courage in oneself; rather, it complements the quality of courage as being authentic. That is precisely because fear leads one to improve herself in her endless act of "accumulation of righteousness." This also shows how devastating Mencius's critique of Gaozi is: he is saying that Gaozi's "unmoved mind," or his "confidence of righteous-

---

49   Zhu, *Sishu zhangju jizhu*, 229.

ness" might be delusional given that he pays no heed to the necessity of self-examination.

This interpretation echoes Confucius's expression, "to know being shameful (*chi*) is akin to courage." Indeed, *chi*-shame is not equivalent to the virtue of courage (勇). However, the *chi* functions as a guide for self to cultivate its willingness to engage in constant self-examination, and then gradually helps it build up an authentic courage, which in turn guides the self to properly remain confident in being responsible and in doing what is meant by righteousness.

Thus, we have seen the whole picture of the function of *chi* based on our interpretation of *Mengzi* 2A2. First, given that *chi*-shame is accompanied by an assessment of ethical self-image in accordance with an awareness of moral responsibility, the shame in this context can lead a person to engage in moral self-examination. Second, through the continuous process of self-examination, the person will internalize the practical idea of "righteousness," instead of dogmatically imitating its form. Third, as the self keeps reminding itself of the importance of self-examination, it refrains from expecting that it can be free of *chi*-shame, and thereby its gradual "accumulation of righteousness" improves its practical knowledge of what is righteousness and how to embody that moral ideal. Lastly, as a result of this process, the self can mindfully build up a moral courage, thus remaining confident in fulfilling her responsibiblity for herself, others, and all things.

Conclusion

This paper has explored the semantics of *chi*-shame to evaluate its importance in the classical Confucian context. I have argued that it should be distinguished from another sense of shame (*xiu*), which is often used as a label for describing Chinese culture as a shame-culture. The basis of this argument is that *chi* necessarily implies the sense of "guilt" unlike *xiu*. What I have hoped to achieve through this differentiation of *chi* from *xiu* is essentially to highlight the distinct significance of *chi* for the moral self-cultivation, which is indispensable for realizing the Confucian idea of moral righteousness. Chinese studies of moral sentiments in the Confucian texts tend to highlight the function of "empathy" (*burenren zhi xin* 不忍人之心), evolving around the discourse of "benevolence" (*ren* 仁). I must admit the emotion of *chi* is secondary to empathy (*burenren*), since without it, the sense of responsibility would be groundless. But we must ask ourselves if we can sufficiently ground morality solely on the basis of empathy.

This question is left unresolved at the end of this article. However, we should further investigate whether or not empathy needs to be supplemented by something else like *chi*-shame if we are to develop a more realistic and intersubjectively responsible framework of ethical judgment. Certainly, I am not the first one to point out the detailed interpretation of the Confucian *ren*. Chen Shaoming has distinguished two kinds of empathy.[50] On the one hand, it could simply represent a sympathetic concern without giving any reflection of responsibility. For instance, when seeing a sudden fall of a child into a well, we could demonstrate this type of sympathy.[51] On the other, it could be tied to an intense self-reflection of responsibility as we might detect in the case like King Xuan's famous response to the sacrifice of an innocent ox.[52] If Confucius's greatness lies in his teaching of benevolence, then, Chen further argues, Mencius's contribution lies in his illustration of *ren* in light of righteousness (*yi* 義). This chapter has shown that righteousness, according to Mencius, indeed grows in accord with the proper exercise and self-reflective understanding of *chi*-shame.

---

50 Shao-Ming Chen, "Between Benevolence and Righteousness," *Philosophical Research*, 11 (2012): 32–40.

51 In *Mengzi* 2A6.

52 In *Mengzi* 1A7.

References

Benedict, Ruth. *The Chrysanthemum and The Sword*. United States of America: Houghton Mifflin Company, 1989.

Bloom, Irene. *Mencius*. Edited by Philip J. Ivanhoe. New York: Columbia University Press, 2009.

Chan, Wing-Tsit. *A Source Book In Chinese Philosophy*. New Jersey: Princeton University Press, 1963.

Chen, Shao-Ming. "A Phenomenological Analysis of Shame." *Philosophical Research*, no. 12 (2006): 100–107.

_____. "Between Benevolence and Righteousness." *Philosophical Research*, no. 11 (2012): 32–40.

Geaney, Jane. "Moral Boundaries: Shame in Early Confucianism." *Philosophy East and West* 54, no. 2 (2004): 113–42.

Lamb, R.E. "Guilt, Shame, and Morality." *Philosophy and Phenomenological Research* 43, no. 3 (1983): 329–46.

Legge, James, trans. "Gong Sun Chou I." In *Chinese Text Project*, n.d. https://ctext.org/mengzi/gong-sun-chou-i/ens.

Legge, James. "Li Ren." In *Chinese Text Project*, n.d. https://ctext.org/analects/li-ren/ens.

_____. "Tai Bo." In *Chinese Text Project*, n.d. https://ctext.org/analects/tai-bo/ens.

Liu, JeeLoo. "Wang Fuzhi (Wang Fu-Chich)." In *Encyclopedia of Chinese Philosophy*, edited by Antonis S. Cua, 748–55. New York: Rouledge, 2003.

Norden, Bryan W. Van. "Mencius on Courage." *Midwest Studies in Philosophy*, no. 21 (1997): 237–57.

_____. *Readings in Classical Chinese Philosophy*. Edited by Philip J. Ivanhoe. New York: Seven Bridge Press, 2001.

_____. "The Emotion of Shame and the Virtue of Righteousness in Mencius." *Dao: A Journal of Comparative Philosophy* 2, no. 1 (2002): 45–77.

Nussbaum, Martha C. *Hiding from Humanity: Disgust, Shame, and the Law*. Princeton and Oxford: Princeton University Press., 2004.

Rainey, Lee. "Mencius and His Vast, Overflowing Qi (Hao ran zhi qi)." *Monumenta Serica*, no. 46 (1998): 91–104.

Roetz, Heiner. *Confucian Ethics of the Axial Age*. Albany: State University of New York Press, 1993.

Sakuta, Keiichi. "A Reconsideration of the Culture of Shame." Translated by Kimiko Yagi and Meridith Mckinney. *Review of Japanese Culture and Society* 1, no. 1 (1986): 32–39.

Seok, Bongrae. "Moral Psychology of Shame in Early Confucian Philosophy." In *Reconceptualizing Confucian Philosophy in the 21st Century*, edited by X Yao,

117–49. Singapore: Springer Nature Singapore Pte Ltd. and Higher Education Press, 2017.

Stocker, Michael. "Shame and Guilt." Edited by Paul Bloomfield, 281–303. New York: Oxford University Press, 2008.

Tang, Junyi. *On Education (Yuan-Jiao-Pian)*. On Education (Yuan-Jiao-Pian). Fundamental Exposition of Chinese Philosophy (Zhong-guo-zhe-xue-yuan-lun). Beijing: Zhonghua Shehui Kexue Chubanshe, 2006.

Wang, Fuzhi. *A Contemporary Interpretation of the Meaning of the Four Books*. Vol. 8. Chuan-shan-quan-shu. Hu Nan: Yuelu Shushe, 1988.

_____. *Discourse on Reading the Great Collection of Commentaries on the Four Books*. Beijing: Zhonghua Shuju, 1975.

Williams, Bernard. *Shame and Necessity*. Berkeley: University of California Press, 1993.

Zhu, Xi. *Collected Commentaries on the Four Books (Sishu Zhangju Jizhu)*. Beijing: Zhonghua Shuju, 1983.

Taisuke Ueno

THE FLOWER AS ENCOUNTERING
The Ultimate Goal for the Emptiness of An Actor's Subjectivity in Zeami's Performance Theory

1. *Introduction*

It has been often discussed that Zeami Motokiyo (世阿弥元清 ca. 1363–ca. 1443) verbalized the process of controlling a disobedient body and thereby acquiring high-level acting techniques. By analyzing the idea of "dominance" (*u-shu-fū* 有主風) in the documents written by Zeami, Nishihira Tadashi argues that Zeami assumed an argument concerning double-layered subjectivity: after an actor has achieved a high-level performance well enough to impersonate a character in a Nō drama unconsciously, he must then trace his performance techniques consciously, thus renewing his subjectivity.[1] The double-layered subjectivity described by Nishihira comprises the conscious condition that an actor tries to impersonate the character and the unconscious activity whereby he does not care about how to behave as the character in the drama. Nishihira argues that Zeami discovered this notion of double-layered subjectivity by writing on and then reflecting on his inner awareness of his activity. Nishihira, therefore, focuses on the topic of subjectivity as elucidated in Zeami's book. Although several philosophical interpretations of Zeami's performance theory have addressed his account of subjectivity, especially in relation to so-called emptiness (*mushin* 無心), Nishihira has clarified the more prominent status of the Nō actor. His research has been held in high esteem as a valuable study of Zeami's performance theory from a philosophical perspective.

---

1   Nishihira Tadashi, *Zeami no keiko tetsugaku* (Zeami's Practice Philosophy) (Tokyo: Tokyo University Press, 2009), 175–6. It is generally considered that most Nō actors were male in the medieval age in Japan. Therefore, this paper has used the pronoun "he."

On the other hand, what seems to be lacking is the indigenous viewpoint that the Nō performance is related to religious rituals. Zeami's theory has allowed us to frame performance in view of aesthetics, that is, from a Western philosophical standpoint. Nevertheless, he also made dubious affirmations, like the following:

> The [Nō] performance as we know it today originates when Shōtoku Taishi (聖徳太子) ordered Hada no Kōkatsu (秦河勝) to hold the feast called *sarugaku* (申楽), including sixty-six programs to pray for the safety of the realm (*tenka* 天下) and the satisfaction of the spectators. From that time until the present, people have borrowed the natural scenery as the medium of this performance. Later, that Kōkatsu's far offspring has succeeded this performance, becoming a member of the clergy in Kasuga (春日) and Hie (日吉) shrines.[2]

In several books, Zeami repeatedly explains the origin of Nō, which was also called *sarugaku* during his time. Most philological studies have not dealt with his account of the derivation of Nō in a serious manner because there has not been any historical evidence to support it. Most philosophical studies, including Nishihira's, also have not dealt with this issue because they have been more interested in Western philosophical themes. The concept of double-layered subjectivity is influenced by the Izutsu Toshihiko scheme, which concerns the way to analyze the thought structure in terms of articulation/non-articulation.[3] This dualism has clarified the whole frame of Zeami's obscure thought, and by doing this it has excluded the indigenous, dubious, unenlightened elements. It is significant to situate the actor's subjectivity theory into Zeami's context of the goal of the Nō performance, namely, the "flower" (*hana* 花).

---

2   *Fūshikaden*, 14. I quote Zeami's texts from *Nihon shisō taikei, Zeami, Zenchiku* (Complete Works of Zeami and Zenchiku) and translation is my own. However, in the quoted references, I will leave the titles in the original.

3   Nishihira, 238. According to Nishihira's comprehension, Izutsu described the characteristic of the structure of Eastern thoughts as follows: usually we articulate the world by using words, however, in Yoga, Buddhism, Zen, Taoism etc., we should be driven into the non-articulated worlds—such as emptiness—by practice. Based on this discussion, Nishihira assumed the existence of a dual status world beyond the non-articulated one; this dual status world includes both the articulated and non-articulated world simultaneously.

This paper illustrates the essence of the "flower" by reconsidering the relation between the subjectivity of the practice theory and the origin of the Nō performance, both described in Zeami's works. The paper focuses on the subjectivity from its emergence to its vanishing. Moreover, it clarifies the meaning of the story of the derivation of the Nō performance as practice theory.

2. *Developing subjectivity*

The first thing Zeami notices is that an actor proceeds from an unconscious performance to a conscious one. Zeami describes the ultimate goal of this practice as fulfilling the "flower" through the Nō performance. The "flower," especially the "authentic flower" (*makoto no hana* まことの花), is one of the essential ideas in his theory. This section will describe the relationship between the subjectivity of an actor and the concept "flower." For this, it is necessary to examine the context of *Fūshikaden* (風姿花伝), which describes the moment before an actor realizes the "authentic flower." This book of Zeami's has become known as the first practice theory he wrote.

According to Chapter one, which explains the steps of the practice by age (*Nenrai Keiko* 年来稽古), Nō performers should start their training at seven years of age:

> First, in our performance, an actor generally begins to practice at seven years of age. By training around this age, an actor reveals his gifted performances when he practices something spontaneously. [...] A master should let the child perform anything as a child intends to do (*kokoro no mama ni* 心のままに).[4]

Zeami states that a master can ascertain the talent of a pupil from his raw performance as a child actor. He also mentions that a master should not tell the student whether his acting was good or bad because he would lose motivation, as his Nō performance would not improve anymore. At this age, a child is not aware of what he is or even does. However, the last line of the previous quotation does not mean that, in childhood, an actor performs without any intention:

---

4   *Fūshikaden*, 15.

he follows only his mind; yet he is not conscious of his heart-mind (*kokoro* 心) status. A master must not instruct such an actor so as to prevent him from realizing the condition in which his heart-mind has captured him in reality.

At the age of twelve or thirteen, an actor becomes aware of his performance. Zeami called this condition "heart-mind adhering" (*kokoro duku* 心づく):

> From around this age, when already the voice [of an actor] gradually reaches the adequate tone, [and he] is also becoming aware of his performance [as a Nō actor], [a master] should teach him some techniques of impersonation, step by step.[5]

The subjectivity of the Nō actor has emerged at this age. Zeami described how an actor of this age seemed to be *yūgen* (幽玄)[6]: his voice is appealing because of his boyhood. In a juvenile actor's performance, spectators tend to see admirable qualities instead of faults. Zeami also claimed that a master must not burden the boy with many delicate impersonation techniques. The reason must be that it is unnatural for a pupil to play a character skillfully: an atmosphere that a pupil is forced to act by following his master's way. Although a pupil has yet to apprehend his genuine heart-mind, the subjectivity of the Nō performer grows inwardly over time. "The flower he possesses at this age is not the authentic flower (*makoto no hana* まことの 花), but just a transitory one (*jibun no hana* 時分の花)," noted Zeami. This implies a process of recognizing the actor's genuine heart-mind, but also the necessity to abandon it.

An actor finds his genuine heart-mind when he is confronted with a standstill, where his performance does not satisfy the spectators. Regarding the practice of a seventeen or eighteen-year-old, Zeami says the following:

---

5   *Fūshikaden*, 15.
6   The nuance of the aesthetic term *yūgen* depended on the author of that period. Zeami illustrates it as follows: "For example, in a person, court lady (*nyōgo* 女 御), higher position lady in court (*kōi* 更衣), or prostitute, beautiful lady, brilliant gentleman, in vegetation, variety of flowers, the figure of such things is *yūgen*" (*Fūshikaden* 50).

As soon as an actor's voice has transformed, the younger flower has disappeared. His figure turns top-heavy, loses elegant flowing shapes, since the age when he had an enchanting flowering voice, and acted readily has passed; [now] he has to change his performance style suddenly and will lose motivation. As a result, [he] gives up practicing at this age [...] because the spectators seem to perceive his performance as strange.[7]

Adolescence generally exposes secondary sexual characteristics such as voice change and figure transformation, thus the challenge presented to actors is how to deal with these bodily changes. However, this period is significant from the perspective of realizing his subjectivity: "At this age, he must continue to practice, but he also has to realize that this is the boundary determining whether or not he will be successful and whether to abandon Nō performance for the rest of his life."[8] Facing this adversity calls upon one's subjectivity. If an actor gives up his practice, "Nō performance will stop."[9] Thus, he discovers his heart-mind or subjectivity at this stage of his life as an actor.

An actor's voice and body become stable around the ages of twenty-four to twenty-five. Simultaneously, he becomes arrogant. When he competes with a famous elder performer, he may sometimes outshine the veteran. But this arrogant display is inefficient for the young actor, as success leads him to mimic complicated techniques, as if he is already an accomplished actor. Hence, he adopts an inappropriate attitude for the authentic way of Nō performance. Zeami, pointing out that this is a transitory success, states the following: "Therefore, your mind—in which you mistake a transitory flower for the authentic one—is the cause of your being very far from the genuine one."[10] Zeami reproaches the actor's arrogant attitude and emphasizes that an actor must realize where to situate himself appropriately. This involves an actor recognizing his genuine heart-mind discovered during the troubles of his teenage years.

---

7   *Fūshikaden*, 16.
8   *Fūshikaden*, 16.
9   *Fūshikaden*, 16.
10   *Fūshikaden*, 17.

Following such an ordeal, Zeami repeats the phrase "the favor of the public" (*tenka no yurusare* 天下の許され)[11] in the section that discusses actors of thirty-four to thirty-five years old:

> If an actor acquires and realizes the previous mystiques [...] he will certainly obtain the favor of the public and must be a popular actor, [...]; if an actor does not obtain enough of the public's favor at this age [...] we should judge him as an actor who has not achieved the authentic flower.[12]

Zeami noted that if an actor does not flourish at this age, it would be evident that he is not a performer possessing the authentic flower, even though he may be skillful. He emphasized that the level of one's Nō performance will decline after his forties, except for experts. Thus, in his description of actors in their mid-forties, Zeami advises them to pay attention to health decline, to situate their successors in the main parts of performances, and to perform other roles more readily. Yet he argues that, "if the flower has not disappeared at this age, it must have been the authentic one."[13] It is significant to consider the reason Zeami used the phrase "must have been (*hazu bekere* はずべけれ)" in the previous quotation. He was around thirty-eight years old when he finished writing the archetype of *Fūshikaden*, the so-called *Kaden* (花伝). As such, he was unaware of what lay ahead in his future as an actor. This implies that Zeami likely wrote these articles thinking of his dead father, Kanami Kiyotsugu 観阿弥清次 (1333–1384), who had passed away at fifty-two, when Zeami was around twenty-two years of age. The time of Kanami's death lines up with the fact that Chapter one of *Fūshikaden* ends with the description of the actor in his fifties. The last part of the chapter one nostalgically depicts the scene of his father's performance: "if an actor becomes an accomplished one, the flower will remain in his performances." It is essential

---

11   The term *tenka* usually refers to the real world, or to the political realm. In Japanese, however, the character *ten* 天 originally connotes the celestial field where the deities, including Amaterasu, live. Thereby, in a certain sense, we might interpret Zeami's concept more broadly: the power of Amaterasu bestows the favor of the public on the actor. Further explanation will be provided later.

12   *Fūshikaden*, 18.

13   *Fūshikaden*, 19.

here to confirm that the origin of the "authentic flower," according to Zeami, was the performance of his dead father.

From the perspective of the discovery of one's subjectivity, the practice theory in *Fūshikaden* Chapter one can be described as follows: first, there is no self-consciousness at the beginning of Nō performance practice in seven years old boys. Next, by the age of seventeen, an actor faces the trouble of voice and body development; but it is also when he achieves his subjectivity as a Nō performer. From that moment on, the actor must overcome this suffering to develop subjectivity. Yet, he might fall into the trap of arrogance unless he is aware of his actual level of skill.

3. *Vanishing subjectivity*

Although Zeami seems to have emphasized the development of subjectivity in *Fūshikaden* Chapter one, he would later hold that it was *emptiness* that brought out the appearance of a genuine Nō performance. This involves the subjectivity of the actor possessing the authentic flower and the process of practice as described by Zeami. *Fūshikaden*, which is today one of the most famous practice theories of Zeami, was at first named *Kaden*. Through the process of editing for approximately twenty-five years (from the age of thirty-eight to sixty-two), Zeami added several sections and renamed the text *Fūshikaden*. Despite new content being added over the years, most of Chapter one remained unchanged.

As I mentioned previously, Zeami emphasizes the phrase "the favor of the public" in the articles about the actor after the age of thirty-four or five. This phrase appears in Chapter five, "On Mystique" (*Ōgi* 奥義), which was presumably written after he finished Chapter one:

> An actor who has brilliant skills and obtains the favor of the public must effectively perform whatever he must. [...] This performance must be the flower. [...] It is the actor who has reached this [high] level that will obtain the favor of the public, and the spectators—who either lived in the country, far from the capital or in the countryside—must be fascinated [when they watch his performance].[14]

---

14 *Fūshikaden*, 43–44.

Following these quotations, Zeami stated that he wrote *Fūshikaden*
to clarify the mystique of the Nō performance. The term "the favor of
the public" often appears coupled with the idea of *omoshiro* (面白 in
the previous quotations, translated as "effectively" and "fascinated").[15]
In Japanese, the term literally refers to the way that light illuminates
the face in white shades. *Omoshiro* appears in his theory in the following way: for example, in *Fūshikaden* Chapter seven, "The flower,
the fascination (*omoshiro[ki]*), and the freshness, these three have
the same heart-mind."[16] Or, in *Shūgyokutokka* (拾玉得花) that Zeami
wrote later, "the fascination, the flower, and the freshness, these three
are oneness, but they have a different name."[17] These explanations
indicate the close connection between the idea of *omoshiro* and the
"flower," which are the most significant concepts in Zeami's performance theory. On the other hand, in *Kakyō* (花鏡), which Zeami
wrote in parallel when recompiling *Fūshikaden*, he implied a new
level of performance beyond "fascination":

> Furthermore, there is a level beyond fascination (*omoshiro[ki]*), which is when
> the spectators exclaim "Au . . ." unintentionally. This is the level of "impression"
> (感 *kan*). [However,] this is the type of impression where the spectators are not
> even conscious of their enjoyment (*omoshiro*) because they do not have any con-
> sciousness. [...] According to the *I Ching*, the character 咸 alone, a figure that
> removes the heart-mind (心) that constitutes the bottom part of the character
> *kan* (感), was pronounced "kan." This is why the authentic impression must be
> without any feelings.[18]

This quotation describes the spectators' state of being purely
impressed. However, Zeami developed this theory not to describe
the spectators' response but for the actors' use. Hence, it is correct
to assume that he intended to tell his actor successors to perform in

---

15   It is difficult to use a fixed translation term for *omoshiro* because this Japanese term
     has ambiguous meanings. Rimer and Yamazaki (1984) translated the same parts as
     follows: "A truly great artist who enjoys the genuine approbation of his audience
     will be able to perform in all style and make each of them enjoyable." "An actor at
     this higher level of proficiency will be respected everywhere, even by those in the
     countryside and in the far-off provinces" (39–40). Therefore, depending on the
     context, I use several English terms in this paper for the Japanese term *omoshiro*.
16   *Fūshikaden*, 55.
17   *Shūgyokutokka*, 188.
18   *Kakyō*, 95–6.

such a way as to move the spectators without triggering their feelings. Therefore, he adds the following statement to the previous quotation:

> It is the same with the level of an actor. [If] he evolves past the beginner-level, he will be only esteemed as just a good actor [by spectators]. Then, he has already achieved the level of a skillful actor (*jōzu* 上手). There is a higher level beyond this, a so-called distinguished actor level (*meijin* 名人). [However,] there is [even] a more [fascinating] level beyond that: a level where the actor can achieve "impression without any feelings" [on the part of the spectators] and where he obtains "the favor of the public."[19]

It is evident from these two quotations that "the favor of the public" had something to do with "the fascination" (*omoshiro*), and especially with the "impression without any feelings" (*mushin no kan* 無心の感). However, the "impression without any feelings" is the "emptiness" of spectators. From this viewpoint, the phrase "the favor of the public" suggests the spectators' estimation that they are watching a prominent popular performer. An actor who has "the favor of the public" is, namely, a performer who leads spectators to the point of emptiness. The studies on "emptiness" provided by Nishihira have usually focused on merely eliminating the subjectivity of the actor. However, the subjectivity of the actor is affected by the feelings of the spectators. The spectators' "impression without any feelings" implies the strong relationship between the spectators and the actor. We can say that the subjectivity of an actor, in this sense, becomes passive as he practices.

In *Shūgyokutokka*, which indicates the oneness of the fascination (*omoshiro*[*ki*]), the flower, and the freshness (*mezurashi*[*ki*] 珍しき), Zeami paraphrases it as the oneness of "elegance (*myō* 妙), the flower, the fascination (*menpaku* 面白)."[20] "The elegance" (or elegant flower *myōka* 妙花) lies at the top level in the nine practice steps in *Kyūi* (九位), which was written at around the same time as Zeami wrote *Shūyokutokka*. According to *Kyūi*, "elegance" expresses the condi-

---

19   *Kakyō*, 96. According to the original texts, the phrase used here is not 天下の許され (*tenka no yurusare*), but 天下の名望 (*tenka no meibō*). However, as far as I interpret this, there is no philosophical difference between them here. Hence, I have used the same phrase in translation.

20   *Menpaku* is another reading of 面白 (*omoshiro*) in Japanese. There is no difference in meaning.

tion of being "without verbalizing, vanishing any heart-mind" (*gongo dōdan, shingyō shometsu* 言語道断、心行諸滅). It means that not only the spectators but also the actor is unable to express his impressions in words. In other words, neither have any feelings in their heart-mind when they are immersed in such an elegant performance. We can comprehend it more specifically as follows:

> The "impression without any feelings" of the spectators and the "elegant flower" have the same meaning. Nonetheless, it acquires the *u-shu-fū* (有主風) only at that level which is authentic and effortless (*shinjitsu no yasuki kurai* 真実の安き位).[21]

Here, *u-shu-fū* ties together the relationship between the "impression without any feelings" and the "elegant flower." In Japanese, this term includes the literal meaning of becoming the master of one's performance. According to the work, the actor who finally acquires mystique through practices—as described in chapters of *Kaden* (*Nenrai Keiko* 年来稽古, *Monomane* 物学, *Mondō* 問答, *Besshi* 別紙),[22] *Shikadō* (至花道), and *Kakyō* (花鏡)—can impersonate any character as he intends (*kokoro no mama* 心のまま), without challenge. Although this level is very high, Zeami emphasizes that it is not the ultimate level because the actor still acts on his intentions. It is similar to the performance of the seven-year-old in terms of subjectivity. As long as the actor acts on the basis of his subjectivity, even if he can perform the character effortlessly and impress the spectators, Zeami did not consider that such an actor had reached the highest level. There was an ultimate condition with nothing in one's mind. It is the authentic, effortless level where the actor acquires the *u-shu-fū*.

Zeami put forth his thoughts about *u-shu-fū* mainly in *Shikadō*. As long as an actor learned dancing (*mai* 舞) and singing (*utai* 謡) by impersonating his master, his level is still *mu-shu-fū* (無主風). The idea of *mu-shu-fū* is an antonym of *u-shu-fū*. In Japanese, the term refers to the condition that an actor has not become the master of his performance yet. Specifically, an actor seems to impersonate only the

---

21   *Shūgyokutokka*, 189.
22   According to philological studies, the archetype of *Fūshikaden* comprised these four titles.

superficialities of his master: he cannot make his master's techniques his own. According to the explanation by Zeami, what is worse, such an actor cannot improve his performance anymore. It comes to be evident that he has stayed at the *mu-shu-fū* level:

> To impersonate and learn very well the performance that a master played, gaze away and replicate, make it his own, ingrain it into his own body and soul, and finally become an expert who can perform anything unchallenged: this level is *shu* (主). It is a living Nō performance. The actor who achieved the *u-shu-fū* level must be the person who utilizes his fundamental ability for his practice, rapidly acquires the matters that he has learned and practiced so far, and then becomes the character itself.[23]

In this quotation, there is a clue to understanding *u-shu-fū*. According to the last line, the practices which lead an actor to the *u-shu-fū* result in "becoming the character." We usually express this condition in Japanese with the construction *ni naru* (になる). As such, in *Shūgyokutokka*, the authentic and effortless level (真実の安き位) that is closely related to the idea *u-shu-fū* signifies the condition of becoming the character itself.

To comprehend it more clearly, it is helpful to compare two Japanese constructions, *wo suru* (をする) and *ni naru* (になる).[24] In general, practice means learning and impersonating the techniques of the actor's master until he can perform as he intends. In other words, an actor has many assignments to acquire the elements which were shown by his master. He attempts to ingrain them into his body and soul through everyday practice. In this case, there is a distance between the object to be learned and the subject of an actor. We describe this condition with *wo suru* in Japanese. By contrast, the more an actor practices something repeatedly, the more he can perform it spontaneously. Training gradually removes the difficulty in impersonating something. Finally, he will be able to act out unconsciously whatever he has practiced. The boundary between the object and the subject then disappears. We describe this condition with *ni naru* in Japanese. Hence, if an actor feels something diffi-

---

23 *Shikadō*, 114.
24 Cf., Ueno Taisuke. *Hana tsutō Hana* (Transmission from flower to flower). Kyōto: Kōyō shobō, 2017.

cult in his performance, this implies that he has been in the *wo suru* condition because the object and subject are not one; if he does not feel any obstacles, this signifies the *ni naru* condition because the object and subject are nearing oneness. Taking the above reasoning into account, we can clarify the actor's path to emptying his subjectivity. The authentic and effortless level of achieving the *u-shu-fū* means ultimately to fall into the *ni naru* condition, like the expression "becoming the character" suggests.

On the other hand, how about the relationship between the actor and the spectators? According to the description in *Kyūi*, the condition of the elegant flower, which fulfills no words and no heart-mind, applies not only to the actor, but also to the spectators. In this sense, the highest performance has the mysterious power to lead the spectators into the state of "impression without any feelings." It means that the spectator's subjectivity also leans on the actor's performance. Furthermore, in this state, no one maintains subjectivity. What happens in such a situation of emptiness?

The previous quotation is relevant to answering this question. Zeami argued that when a prominent expert impersonates the character without difficulty, "a living Nō" has appeared. This message has a significant meaning. It implies that the vitalized Nō manifests itself through the emptiness of the actor and the spectators. In other words, the performance of the actor's vanishing subjectivity gives life to Nō itself through the abandonment of the heart-mind of the spectators. However, it is not the intention or tactic of the actor to bring the spectators into this state of "impression" because there is no subjectivity there. It is the Nō itself that fulfills the performance if one manages to put into words such an indescribable condition suggested by Zeami.

Although we understood that the emptiness of the actor and the spectators made "the living Nō" appear, this explanation has something to do with the fundamental understanding of Nō itself, as Zeami supposed.

4. *The origin theory of* sarugaku *performance*

In *Shūgyokutokka*, Zeami restated the effect of "fascination" (*omoshiro*) with reference to the evolution of the Nō performance:

> First of all, the origin of the name "*omoshiro*" [is the following:] at the *Ama no Kagu* mountain (天香久山), [the deities] enjoyed the performance of *kagura* (*kagura no yūgaku* 神楽の遊楽): when Ōnkami[25] (大神) opened the stone door of the cave, the faces (*omote* 面) of the deities could turn luminous. This was the first instance of *omoshiro*.[26]

Though there are various types of stories like this, this kind of myth is well-known as the *Ama no Iwato* legend in Japan. According to the general understanding, Susanowo no Mikoto raided Amaterasu Ōmikami (天照大神).[27] Amaterasu rushed into the cave at *Ama no Kagu* mountain to escape from his violence. Suddenly, it became dark because Amaterasu was the sun deity. Trying to lure her out, the other gods planned to play performances in front of the cave entrance where she had shut herself. They considered that if Amaterasu was interested in the outside orgy, she must open the stone door by herself. As the deities expected, when they began to perform for Amaterasu, she opened the door. The world then recovered the sunlight. The evolution of *omoshiro* is often associated with this episode. That is because in Japanese, the term *omo* means face, while *shiro* refers to the color white: therefore, as soon as Amaterasu opened the stone door, the faces of the deities turned bright.

In addition to that, Zeami connected this etymological description to the performance theory in *Shūgyokutokka*. Zeami considered that the moment when Amaterasu came out of the cave was not *omoshiro*. According to his interpretation, at that moment, "[the deities] were only conscious of pleasure," which "must have been delightful." He

---

25   Nowadays, this term is pronounced as "Ōmikami." However, in the medieval age, it was pronounced as "Ōnkami."

26   *Shūgyokutokka*, 188.

27   To this day, most Japanese people think of Amaterasu as a goddess. However, this fixed image has been changing after modernization. In the premodern age, there were various explanations regarding the sexuality of Amaterasu. I have used the female pronoun as a matter of convenience since there is no clue as to how Zeami would have considered it.

classified this situation into three phases: the first phase is "the elegance"—the deities could not express anything because of the darkness. The second phase is "the flower"—Amaterasu opened the stone door, and simultaneously the sunlight illuminated across the world. The third phase is "the fascination" (*omoshiro*)—the deities realized that the sun god Amaterasu illuminated their faces once again.

Takemoto Mikio has pointed out that Zeami referred to an episode in *Kogoshūi* (古語拾遺) for this etymological explanation.[28] Furthermore, we can identify a Zen Buddhist influence on his theory, which probably derived from the teachings of Kiyō Hōshū (岐陽方秀 ca.1361–1424) or from Fugan Temple (補巌寺), where he renounced the world at the age of sixty.[29] However, these studies hardly give adequate accounts for the reason Zeami used the metaphor of the *Ama no Iwato* legend. Of course, it is possible to presume that his explanations were just rhetorical. Nevertheless, I will attempt to interpret it by situating this legend according to his performance theory. There are two significant points. Firstly, there are several articles discussing the Amaterasu legend in Zeami's performance theory. Secondly, these are often related to the explanation he gives about the evolution of the Nō performance. At the beginning of *Fūshikaden*, he writes:

> Fundamentally, inquiring into the origin of the Nō performance—which has the power to lead people to live longer (*sarugaku ennen* 申楽延年)—some said that it originated from the place where Buddha had lived, while others said that it derived from the age of the deities. Nonetheless, time has passed, and eons have flown by. It is impossible to imitate such old styles of performance.[30]

In this quotation, Zeami recognized the age of the deities as one of the origins of the Nō performance. After this statement, he pointed

---

28 Zeami, *Fūshikaden Sandō*, ed., Takemoto Mikio (Tōkyō: Kadokawa Gakugei Shuppan, 2009).

29 It is unknown where Zeami learned such Zen Buddhist knowledge. According to *Shikishō* 史記抄, which was written by Tōgen Zuisen 桃源瑞仙 (1430–1489), Zeami often participated in the lectures held by Kiyō Hōshū. Furthermore, Zeami was also close with the second chief monk Chikusō Chigon (竹窓智巌) of Fugan Temple in present-day Nara prefecture (where Zeami and his wife donated several paddy fields, according to the temple's register). It is not inconceivable that Chikusō Chigon could have taught him the essence of Zen Buddhism.

30 *Fūshikaden*, 14.

to the legend of Prince Shōtoku and Hada no Kōkatsu as the historical origin of the current Nō performance. Although I quoted this part in the Introduction, I will also briefly summarize it here: during the era of emperor Suiko, Prince Shōtoku ordered Hada no Kōkatsu to hold a feast, including sixty-six types of programs to pray for the safety of the realm (*tenka anzen* 天下安全) and satisfaction of the people (*shonin keraku* 諸人快楽). This was called *kagura* (神楽). Priests of Zeami's age from the Kasuga and Hie shrines were also performers, and they took over this *kagura* stream. The signature *Hada no Moto-kiyo* (秦元清) used by Zeami in the last line of *Fūshikaden* Chapter three signifies that he believed strongly in this origin story. According to his idea, Nō performance had continued from the sixty-six feasts in which Kōkatsu performed.

We can see that Zeami had already associated the idea *omoshiro* with this origin story: both in the first edition of Chapter seven of *Kaden*, which is known as one of the oldest manuscripts written by Zeami, and at the beginning of *Fūshikaden* Chapter four. Here, I quote from the latter:

> First, about *sarugaku* (申楽): during the beginning of the age of gods, when Amateru Ōnkami closed herself in the stone cave, the world (*tenka* 天下) became dark everlastingly. All the deities (*yaoyorozu no kami* 八百万の神) assembled at the *Ama no Kagu* mountain to make the Ōnkami return to a good mood, so they began performing the *kagura*, which included singing, dancing, and impersonating a jocular man [to pray to Ōnkami]. [...] Listening to the outside voices a little, [Ōnkami] slightly opened the stone door. Then, light returned to the land. The faces (*omo* 面) of the deities turned white (*shiro* 白). The performance at that time is the beginning of *sarugaku*, and so on.[31]

At the time he described this evolution in *Fūshikaden*, he must have never considered a threefold explanation like that given in *Shūgyokutokka*. However, it is easy for us to find the elements of the story of the Nō origin and "the fascination" (*omoshiro*) from here. There is an extricable relationship between the Nō origin legend and the concept of *omoshiro*, which is the essence of "the flower." It could be said that Zeami made use of this derivation episode not for legitimizing his performance but for exemplifying his theory. To supple-

---

31   *Fūshikaden*, 38.

ment this perspective, I will bring more evidence from two different perspectives. One is the etymology of the Nō performance itself; the other is the plot of Zeami's works.

Firstly, in the same chapter of *Fūshikaden*, Zeami analyzed the origin of Nō performance etymologically:

> Prince Shōtoku (Jōgū Taishi 上宮太子), because of the declining period, removed the left part of 神 (god *kami*) of the Chinese character but left the right one. [He] named this [Kōkatsu] performance *sarugaku* (申楽), because this Chinese character figured the shape 申 (monkey *saru*), which was a character in the [Japanese Zodiac] calendar. It is because of devoting the pleasure [to the deities][32] or having been derived from *kagura* (神楽).[33]

It is not significant whether his etymological explanation accords with the historical or philological ones. Moreover, although some studies have been suspicious of whether Zeami himself wrote this explanation or not because of differences in the writing style, that is also not significant. The truth is that he certainly included this explanation in *Fūshikaden*. Namely, even if other people created this explanation, Zeami basically admitted it. Moreover, there exists another record where he explained the Nō derivation to Kiyō Hōshū.[34] These statements provide sufficient evidence to say that Zeami believed that his performance had something to do with *kagura*. He emphasized this nexus coherently from *Kaden* to *Shūgyokutokka*. Although some studies have labeled this etymological explanation as ridiculous

---

32   In the original text, Zeami used here the construction *tanoshimi wo mōsu* (楽しみを
       申す). It means "to convey the pleasure (楽) to persons who are ranked higher than
       the teller." In Japanese, the Chinese character 申 includes the meaning of "telling"
       or "conveying" a story to beings worthy of respect.

33   *Fūshikaden*, 39.

34   Tōgen Zuisen wrote about this in retrospect, as he had heard it from another
       monk, in *Shikishō*. "A long time ago, [Zeami] stated [the following:] usual usage
       has been excessively distorted. Our performance has been called Sarugaku (猿
       楽 monkey performance): this name is out of the question. There is no evidence
       that [猿楽] has turned into 申楽. Furthermore, [we do not admit the opinion that
       people used] a character 猿 (monkey) [at first]. This [performance] was essentially
       kagura (神楽). People [at first] used 申, which omitted the right part of the first
       letter of character 神, gradually [people changed] the character 申 into 猿." Though
       the sound 猿 is the same as 申 in Japanese, there are differences between them. The
       former is more vulgar than the latter.

or the phrase as merely legitimizing his Nō performance as superior to others,[35] we can situate it as part of the philosophy of his performance. Thus, the point here is the connection between these derivation stories and the theory of vanishing subjectivity.

It is relevant to survey his *kagura* image in his works. Zeami wrote not only performance theories but also more than sixty plays. From these plays, we can comprehend the effectiveness of *kagura*. There are several plays that deal with praying to the deity called Kami Nō (神能), which was performed just after the Okina performance (翁) during Zeami's time. In *Oimatsu* (老松), which has remained one of the well-known plays in Kami Nō to this day, Zeami depicted a typical *kagura* performance. I summarize the story before examining the *kagura*: Umezu no Nanigashi (梅津の某) went to Anrakuji temple in Dazaifu because he had a revelatory dream that he must go there if he believed firmly in the Heavenly god of Kitano (Kitano Tenjin). He encountered two men: one was older and protected the forest, while the other younger one guarded the flowers. Umezu inquired where "the flying plum branch" (*tobiume* 飛び梅) was located.[36] According to the legend, as soon as the older man introduced it to him, he disappeared into the pine by the plum, together with the younger man. Later, Umezu heard that they were the deities of the pine and the plum that served Kitano Tenjin. He decided to wait for the reappearance of the two gods. Then, when the older god reappeared, he began to devote the "God Kagura" (Kami Kagura 神神楽) to the Heavenly god to pray for the everlasting reign of the current emperor.[37] At the

---

35 See for instance, Omote Akira. "Zeami no 'Sarugaku (サルガク) = 申楽 setsu' o megutte: *Fūshikaden* dai yon shingihen' no seiritunendai sonota" (On Zeami's explanation that Sarugaku Equals 申楽: *Fūshikaden* Chapter four, etc."), Nōgaku kenkyū18 (1994): 1–48.

36 There was a well-known legend in Japan regarding this. In the past, Sugawara no Michizane (菅原道真) was suddenly relegated to Dazaifu on Kyūshū island from the capital because he was a rival of the Fujiwara clan, who was at the center of politics. Just after that, mysteriously, the plum and pine that Michizane planted and loved in his old homestead flew there to be with their master.

37 In general, it has been considered that this *kagura* performance is devoted not to the Heavenly god, but Umezu. However, in that case, we cannot explain why Umezu heard the voice of the Heavenly god in the last scene. Therefore, in a previous paper (Ueno 2019), I proposed a new interpretation analyzing it from the

end of the performance, the Heavenly god gives them the oracle without the figure.

This means that the Heavenly god corresponded to the "God Kagura" performed by the older deity. In other words, this scene was the epiphany of the Heavenly god that hid from the beginning to the end. Zeami implied in this plot that the "God Kagura" had the significant role of drawing out the god. This effect is similar to the *kagura* in the *Ama no Iwato* legend. According to the *kagura* image of Zeami, it has the power to make deities appear out of their hiding.

Even though there are several articles of dubious description regarding the origin of Nō performance in the practice theory stated by Zeami, it is still necessary to refer to them when discussing his performance philosophy. Situating such suspicious statements into Zeami's widely known Nō performance theory would open the path to finding those indigenous philosophical elements which cannot be fully comprehended solely within the Western philosophical scheme.

5. *Conclusion*

Writings by Zeami demonstrated not only the technical mystique of Nō performance but also the fulfillment of *sarugaku* as *kagura*. In this respect, studies focusing on the emptiness of the actor's subjectivity in Zeami's performance theory become a one-sided interpretation.

The discussion reviews "the impression without any feelings." The "fascination" (*omoshiro*) that the actor with the elegant flower fulfilled does not rely upon his subjectivity in order to impress the spectators intentionally. Neither the actor nor the spectators ultimately have any individualities in "the impression without feelings." Here, the actor does not "perform the character intentionally" (*wo suru* を する), but "becomes the character unconsciously" (*ni naru* になる). Thus, the performance turns into "a living Nō," Zeami maintained. It means that the positions of the Nō itself, and of the actor, reverse. Put another way, although we usually think that the actor plays the

perspective of the similarity between the structure of "God Kagura" and the origin story of Nō performance as stated by Zeami.

Nō performance, it is in fact the Nō that manifests itself through the fulfillment of the actor's performance as if it were vitalized when his subjectivity disappears. This illustration signifies that the Nō comes alive right there, in the moment. In this circumstance, an actor is just the way by which Nō comes into existence. This is why an actor needs to eliminate his subjectivity. This applies not only to the actor but also to the spectators. In Chapter three of *Fushikaden*, for example, Zeami described a situation when many spectators are not fully aware of the Nō performance, as "not all people's minds have turned into Nō yet" (*bannin no kokoro, imada Nō ni narazu* 万人の心、いまだ能にならず).[38] It reveals the essence of success in the Nō performance. Zeami writes it in *Shūgyokutokka* about the landscape where the sunlight revived in this world was brought about by Amaterasu opening the cave door. There is a cardinal element in this description, more than the ordinary idea that the fulfillment of the performance hinges on only the actor's ability: an actor does not just satisfy the spectators with his performance. Taking Zeami's etymological illustration of Nō into account, a *sarugaku* actor plays a role in bringing Amaterasu out of the cave. At that point, the Nō performance leads the spectators into *omoshiro*.

Based on the previous reconsideration of the relation between the disappearance of the subjectivity and the description of the evolution of the Nō performance, it is necessary to redefine the "flower" in Zeami's teachings. Abstract ideas like "the elegant flower" or "the impression without any feelings" are not just conceptual but also real. In *Kyūi*, in which Zeami situates "the elegant flower" on the highest position among the nine practice steps, he describes how the only actor who had achieved everything was his father Kanami, as he told his son Motoyoshi (元能):

[About] our ancestor, Kanami. "The Nō performances of the dance of Shizuka (*shizuka ga mai no Nō* 静が舞の能) or [the impersonation of] the insane woman of the great prayer to Amitābha Buddha in Saga (*saga no dainembutsu* 嵯峨の大念仏) are especially suitable for the ultimate *yūgen* level actor," stated in *Kaden*.

---

38 *Fūshikaden*, 28.

The actor who broke the mountain[39] when he reached the highest flower level broke the mountain when he climbed the middle, which corresponded with dust, and this was done by Kanami alone.[40]

Although these references are naturally considered to be affirmations about his father, such a perspective is not always the case. The point is that Zeami must have recalled his "dead" father at the bottom of his heart when he referred to "the impression without any feelings," even though he must have written it from his own performance experience. The fundamental aspect of his practice theory comprises not only his reflective descriptions but also the reminiscence of the dead man. In other words, if Zeami could achieve the highest performance level like Kanami, in a sense, he would become a Kanami without consciousness. For him, it means that at least he could trace his father's path. His dead father could reincarnate in his body and soul.

This viewpoint touches on the comprehension of "the flower." It should be briefly mentioned that the "flower" appeared in the intersection between Kanami and Amaterasu. Zeami considered that the "flower" was fulfilled when both the actor's and spectator's subjectivity had dissolved into one. Because the "flower" is a different name of *omoshiro*, such a Nō performance simultaneously fulfills *omoshiro* by bringing out Amaterasu from the stone cave. This implies the essence of the "flower": seen from Zeami's personal recollection, it refers not only to the aesthetic concept in his performance theory, but also to the untold encounter with his dead father and Amaterasu; namely, the fulfillment of the "flower" owed to his practice, but also owed to the supernatural being.

The performance of *sarugaku* was not just a theatrical show but a religious ritual.[41] Specifically, the Nō drama describes people encountering the deities or the dead. All the masterpieces attributed to Zeami were related to "praying to Japanese deities for peace" or to "purifying dead souls." It is the reason why the Nō actor should impersonate

---

39   This expression is translated literally along with the original text (*yama wo kuzushi* 山を崩し); it might include the nuance of performing anything easily.

40   *Sarugakudangi*, 264.

41   Sato 2019:250 Zeami. *Fūshikaden*. ed., Satō Masahide. Tōkyō: Chikuma shobō, 2019.

them without his subjectivity. Zeami must have attempted to bring serenity to the public by extracting the deities' power, or he must have endeavored to listen to the regret and resentment of the dead souls by making them appear in the world of the living. Seen from this viewpoint, Kanami was the closest actor to such supernatural beings. The fulfillment of the "flower" in Nō performance means ultimately to encounter them through the vanishing of subjectivities. *Omoshiro* signifies the impact of that.

The practice is then related to the human effort, whereas *kagura* is related to the deities' power. From this perspective, we close our discussion by returning to the first quotation in the Introduction. It is said that Hada no Kōkatsu began to perform several programs "to pray for the safety of the realm and the satisfaction of the spectators." According to this explanation, the essence of the flower reveals itself at the intersection between two elements. In this respect, the theory of emptied subjectivity can connect the description of the origin of Nō performance with "the flower." This study hopes to contribute to a reconsideration of Zeami's performance theory not merely from the abstract philosophical perspective but by drawing attention to his personal philosophical perspective and approach to performance.

References

Zeami. *Nihon shisō taikē, Zeami, Zenchiku* (Complete works of Zeami and Zenchiku). Edited by Omote Akira. Katō, Shūichi. Tōkyō: Iwanami shoten, 1972.

_____. *On the Art of the Nō Drama: The Major Treatises of Zeami*. Translated by J. Thomas Rimer and Yamazaki Masakazu. Princeton: Princeton University Press, 1984.

_____. *Fūshikaden Sandō*. Edited by Takemoto Mikio. Tōkyō: Kadokawa Gakugei Shuppan, 2009.

_____. *Fūshikaden*. Edited by Satō Masahide. Tōkyō: Chikuma shobō, 2019.

Nishihira Tadashi. *Zeami no keiko Tetsugaku* (Zeami's practice philosophy). Tokyo: Tokyo University Press, 2009.

Omote Akira. "Zeami no 'Sarugaku (サルガク) = 申楽 setsu' o megutte: 'Fūshikaden dai yon shingihen' no seiritunendai sonota" (On Zeami's explanation that Sarugaku Equals 申楽: *Fūshikaden* Chapter four, etc."). Nōgaku kenkyū18 (1994): 1–48.

Ueno Taisuke. *Hana tsutō Hana.* (Transmission from flower to flower). Kyōto: Kōyō shobō, 2017.

_____. "Zeami no sarugakuyuraisetsu saikentō: sono shisōtekiganmoku wo megutte." (The reconsideration on the origin description of Sarugaku in Zeami's works: to reveal the aim). Shomotsu shuppan to shakaihenyō (Journal of Books, Publication and Society Transformation] 22 (2019): 83–101.

Acknowledgements

I would like to express my deepest gratitude to Marshall Cody Staton and Alexandra Mustățea for their constructive advice and invaluable help with proofreading and editing this article.

Onur Karamercan

TOPOLOGY OF BALASAGUNİ'S *KUTADGU BİLİG*
Thinking the Between

The nations who once dominated Central Eurasian history—the Scythians and Hsiung-nu, the Huns, Turks, Tibetans, Mongols, Junghars, Manchus, and others—and their descendants disappeared from world historical consciousness for a very long time. Now some of them have reappeared, sometimes under different names, in modern European-style nation-states, and in nearly all cases bereft of any real power. One is entitled to at least ask, "What happened to the old Central Eurasians?" Or to put it wrongly, 'What happened to all the barbarians?'

Christopher I. Beckwith, *Empires of the Silk Road*

1. *Situating* Kutadgu Bilig

1.1. *The Linguistic Place of* Kutadgu Bilig: *Turkic Languages*

KB[1] is the oldest and the longest piece of poetry in all Turkic literatures, being the first Islamic work of literature and philosophy in Turkic languages (more on this below).[2] Yūsuf Balasaguni, the author of *KB*, (1017 or 1019–1070) was born in the city of Balāsāghūn (or

---

1 Throughout the article I abbreviate *Kutadgu Bilig* as *KB*, which will be followed by the number of the couplet and then the page number of the edition that I am consulting in Turkish: cf., Reşid R. Arat, *Kutadgu Bilig:* Metin I (İstanbul: Milli Eğitim Basımevi, 1947). For example, the couple number 950 will be cited as follows: *KB*, 950: 112. Translations from Turkish into English are my own. I also consult Dilaçar's Latin transcription and translation of the Karakhanid Turkic into Modern Turkish: cf., Agop Dilaçar, *Kutadgu Bilig İncelemesi* (Ankara: Türk Dil Kurumu Yayınları, 1995).

2 While one can find many philological, philosophical, linguistic works in Turkish on *KB*, sources are very scarce in English. Assuming that most readers of this essay will find secondary literature in Turkish useless, I find no value in discussing them. See Gulnisa Jamal and Muhammet S. Kafkasyalı, eds., *Kutadgu Bilig Araştırmaları Tarihi* (Ankara: Karınca Yayınları, 2016) for a list of studies done on *KB* in multiple languages.

Balasagun) from which the name Balasaguni derives. Although Bala-saguni started composing *KB* in Balasagun, which is in modern day Kyrgyzstan, he completed it in 1069 in the city of Kaşgar (Kashgar) in the Tarim Basin, which was one of the most important cultural hubs of Central Asia during this period.[3] *KB* is authored in the Karakhanid Turkic, which belonged to the Eastern branch of Turkic languages. At this point, some general information about Turkic languages can be useful to better situate the text in Asian socio-linguistic context.

Turkic languages, which include Turkish, Azeri, Kazakh, Uzbek, Uyghur, Chuvash and Sakha among many others, are considered to be part of the Altaic *sprachbund* that includes vast regions stretching from Southeastern Europe to Northeastern Siberia. Altaic languages include Mongolian and Tungusian languages, and some philologi-cal typologies place Korean and Japanese among a greater Altaic language family, though this view is mostly contested. The discus-sions regarding the origins and classification of Turkic and Altaic languages continue.[4] In general, Altaic languages are neighbored by three language families: Indo-European languages from south, north, and west, Sino-Tibetan languages from south and east, and Semitic languages from southwest. Turkic languages find themselves in one of the linguistically diverse and dynamic regions of the world, being in contact with various historical Chinese, Mongolic, Persian, Indic, Greek, and Arabic languages and literatures. More specifi-cally, Karakhanid Turkic was the language of Karakhanid Khanate, which conquered Transoxiana region along the Silk Road and ruled it over four centuries. Karakhanid Khanate is known to accommodate the Turkic peoples of Karluk origins,[5] that had gradually converted to Islam between the 9th and 10th centuries.[6] While the Karakhanid

---

3   Today the city of Kashgar (喀什) is part of Xinjiang Uyghur Autonomous region in China.

4   For a detailed map and discussion of Turkic languages, see Alexander Savelyev and Martine Robbeets, "Bayesian Phylolinguistics Infers the Internal Structure and the Time-depth of the Turkic Language Family," *Journal of Language Evolution*, 5:1 (2020): 39–53. https://doi.org/10.1093/jole/lzz010

5   Dilaçar, 13.

6   Christopher I. Beckwith, *Empires of the Silk Road: A History of Central Eurasia from the Bronze Age to the Present* (Princeton and Oxford: Princeton University Press, 2009), 167.

Turkic remains similar to Uyghur Turkic, the influence of the Persian language and the introduction of some Islamic vocabulary via Arabic becomes apparent in this period, which displaces religious words and concepts adopted from Buddhism and Manicheism.

1.2. *The Hermeneutic Place of* Kutadgu Bilig: *The Between*

In order to engage with the hermeneutic place from which *KB* emerges in Central Asia, I direct my focus on the idea of the between (Tr: *ara/aralık*), which requires a topological inquiry. From Plato to Nietzsche, various Anglo-European philosophers have placed the human being in the between, often between gods and beasts. In the 20th century, Heidegger famously associated the flowing of the river Ister with Antigone's betweenness as a demi-god among divinities and humans. The notion of the between has drawn considerable attention in contemporary philosophy and place studies from different point of views by scholars such as William Desmond, Nicholas J. Entrikin, and Andrew Mitchell. The idea of the between signifies relationality, connectedness, gatheredness as well as disconnection, difference, and individuality. We are exposed to betweenness more often than we think. Making existential decisions about our lives, such as in cases of the Kierkegaardian either/or, can be conceived of as a situation of the between. The relation between speaking and keeping silent signifies a movement in language that takes place in the between, and so on. However, in existing scholarship, the connection between Central Asian thought and culture and the idea of the between has not been issued in an explicit way, a gap which I will try to fill. My aim is not to put forward a merely metaphysical conception of place, but demonstrate the place-character of a particular place; thus, to show why the topological meaning of the between can be appropriately thought from the between. My thinking in terms of topology, or the logic of place, can be traced between Martin Heidegger's *Topologie des Seins* and Nishida Kitarō's *basho no ronri* (場所の論理). As I unpack the hermeneutic meaning of the between, my understanding of place will also come to the fore. It is against this topological background that the historical, linguistic, and literary place of *KB* comes to the fore.

What does it mean to translate and interpret a literary work from a philosophical standpoint—especially, if the translation at issue is a translation that must travel from a 11th century Central Asian language to 21st century English via modern Turkish? Hermeneutics informs us that when we philosophize, we always do so within the boundaries of a certain historical consciousness, which has been seen as a mode of acquiring self-knowledge.[7] In a certain sense, such a self-knowledge can be formulated as a way of knowing where we stand and how we are situated in our place. In contemporary hermeneutic philosophy, problematizing the situation or the very place of thinking points toward a topological mode of reflection, which suggests an engagement with the ground, ends and horizon of thinking.[8] Thinking through place and places brings us to the domain of a confrontation with history, since history encapsulates the very happening of place and places in time. In other words, history is the *taking place* of time. However, although thinking is always historically-geographically situated, in topological terms it can be argued that any intellectual engagement takes place within the boundaries of a certain language. No thinking can be traced without a language. Language is famously designated by Heidegger as the "house of being," or as the "torture-house of being" by Lacan and "prison-house" by Jameson.[9] Whether we simply are in language, or we are tortured or imprisoned in it, does not change the fact that all that happens to us as human beings first happens in the open-bounded region of language. We bear language; both in the sense of tolerating it, undergoing an experience with it and carrying with us its marks. Nonetheless, a language amounts to more than the uniform language of a designated nation-state: a language always becomes the language that it is through sustained and mostly untraceable dialogues with neighboring languages. It is interesting to note that the Turkish verb *konuşmak* (speak, converse) derives from

---

7   Hans-Georg Gadamer, *Truth and Method*, trans., Joel Weinsheimer and Donald G. Marshall (London and New York: Continuum, 2004), 228.

8   Jeff Malpas, *Heidegger and the Thinking of Place: Explorations in the Topology of Being* (Cambridge, Mass.: The MIT Press, 2012), 20.

9   Martin Heidegger, *On the Way to Language*, trans., P. D. Hertz (New York: Harper & Row Publishers, 1971), 22. ; Slavoj Žižek, "Language, Violence and non-Violence," *International Journal of Zizek Studies*, 2: 3 (2008): 4.

the root of *konmak* (situate, locate), which is also heard in the word *komşu* (*neighbor*).[10] What that implicates is that speaking and conversing is considered to be situated in the nearness of another person or group of persons. Language is not an object, but an act of making neighbors, conversing and inhabiting the same neighborhood with them. To be in language means to be in the between. Central Asia is a region of multiple neighborhoods and *KB* situates right in the *middle* of it.

Differing from the "in-between," the topological sense of betweenness that I would like to underline brings forth the happening of place, which is the "place of existence" (*mekan*), that out of which the edges and the boundaries of place also find their orientation. In the between, places are both jointed and separated, appearing as neighbors that co-determine and transform one another. What that implies is that the between makes empty space (*aralık*) for the emergence of places around it as the places that they are, by providing the room in which they can occur and connect to other places. The between, which Mitchell astutely reformulates as the place of "interpenetration" and "co-belonging,"[11] forms and gathers the boundaries in and through which particular places can be conceived in the same site of nearness. While *ara* is that which relates and brings together two or more entities, *aralık*, as the place of the between, has its own space, in the sense of an interval, the very place of resting. In that context, with the concept of the between I do not simply mean "in-betweenness," which implicates the situation of being encircled by already established poles and centers. Those two are often confused and used interchangeably although they must be distinguished. I argue that the between has its own place, and the regions which connect to it are not fixed points, but are also relative in terms of their own positions. What is at stake is a profoundly enmeshed interconnectivity that signifies a dynamic movement, different from a sense of being fixed and jammed.

---

10   Gerard Clauson, *An Etymological Dictionary of Pre-Thirteenth-Century Turkish* (Oxford: Oxford University Press, 1972), 637; 640.

11   Andrew Mitchell, *The Fourfold: Reading the Late Heidegger* (Evanston: Northwestern University Press, 2015), 121.

2. *Interpreting* Kutadgu Bilig: *The Essence of Language*

KB has been translated into European languages such as German
and English by prominent Turkologists such as A. Vambery and G.
Clauson. Translated most recently into English by Robert Dankoff as
Wisdom of Royal Glory, the title of the book needs some clarifications.
The word *kutadgu* (*kutlu*) conveys a sense of sacred happiness, deriving from the root word of *kut*, which is still used in modern Turkish
in expressions such as *kutlu olsun* to congratulate an anniversary or a
great achievement. Although *bilig* can be interpreted as "knowledge"
in modern Turkish (*bilgi*), this does not say much. Taken together,
kutadgu and *bilig* imply the way of the knowledge toward happiness,
considered sacred and glorious. Within the overall structure of the
book, the notion of knowledge is not necessarily an epistemologi-
cal one, but rather a kind of ethical knowledge of pursuing the good,
explicated through poetic discourse.

Balasaguni's work consists of more than six thousand five hundred
rhyming couplets and eighty-five sections (*bab*), written according to
the Arabo-Persian literary form *masnavi*.[12] The goal of *KB* is to show
to the reader the way towards becoming a good person and attain
happiness and good fate in life through the dialogues of four per-
sonalities.[13] They are Kün-toğdı (Risen Sun), Ay-toldı (Full Moon),

---

12   For a more detailed literary and philological analysis of *KB*, as well as other impor-
     tant literary figures of Turkic literature, see (Dankoff 1983).
13   Since discussing the main narrative does not add much for my elaborations on the
     essence of language, I provide a brief summary here. In a nutshell, Kün-toğdı, as
     the ruler of his state, is in search of a vizier to execute the good and just laws for
     his country who can be a good example of the follower of moral principles for his
     people. Ay-toldı, who learns about this, presents himself to him as a candidate.
     Acknowledging his extraordinary moral virtues, Kün-toğdı appoints Ay-toldı as
     the vizier. When Ay-toldı passes away, Kün-toğdı calls Ay-toldı's son Ögdülmiş
     to his side. Being convinced that Ögdülmiş is capable of replacing his dead father,
     Kün-toğdı appoints him as the new vizier. After his conversations with Ögdülmiş
     and conceiving the difficulties of dealing with the affairs of the state, Kün-toğdı
     decides to hire an adjutant for Ögdülmiş. Ögdülmiş mentions his brother
     Ogdurmış as a candidate, who once took refuge in the mountains to devote his life
     to praying. Despite his various attempts, Ögdülmiş fails to convince Ogdurmış.
     Ogdurmış argues that it would be unacceptable to take up any administrative roles
     for a devout believer like him whose only master can be God. Ögdülmiş visits back
     and forth his brother to receive his good prayers and counsels. One day, he finds

Ögdülmiş (The Praised One), Odgurmış (The Awakened One).[14] Each personality symbolizes a certain moral virtue and an administrative role in the structure of the state and society. According to Balasaguni, these represent the four fundamental "things" (*neñ*) in human existence that allow human beings to arrive at the sacred-glorious happiness. Kün-toğdı, as "the ruler" (*ilig, bey*), characterizes "the just law" (*köni törü*); as the chosen vizier Ay-toldı characterizes "the good fortune, happiness" (*kut*); his son Ögdülmiş, who grows up learning from his father and replaces him characterizes "reason and understanding" (*ukuş*); and his brother Odgurmış, who is a devout and meditative personality, characterizes the human being's longing for the other world and "the end of human existence" (*akıbet*).[15] The work ends with an outstanding epilogue where Balasaguni offers his apologies to his readers, mentioning the limits of his skills as a writer. As we are reminded by Balasaguni in this final section, one of his main goals in the book is to find the right discourse to communicate the wisdom which emerges from pursuing the highest good to the others. This is related to the discussion of the value and meaning of language and reason, especially centered on the idea of authentic speech distinguished from mere discoursing. In that sense, *KB* has both literary and philosophical significations. It is both a work of poetry and philosophy, and it highlights the relationship *between* philosophy and literature through a poetic mode of thinking.

In recent studies on *KB*, while some scholars have found similarities with Plato and Aristotle's ethics,[16] the fact that ideas pertaining to ethics and politics has been expressed via a poetic discourse distinguishes it from its Western equivalents. It must be underlined that *KB* is neither

---

Ogdurmış in bad health. Ogdurmış interprets the meaning of his nightmares for his brother, taking them to be a sign of his approaching death. He delivers his final words about the meaning of life, indicating that one should never be attached to this deceitful world to the point of enslavement. After mourning over the loss of his brother, Ögdülmiş returns to his work and continues to serve Kün-toğdı, trying to bring happiness (*kut*) to his people with the acknowledgement of the limits of human existence.

14   *KB*, 50: 353–358.

15   It is peculiar that the fourth and last personality is the one that designates the human being's being-towards-death, which would obviously have even a more particular sense in languages and literatures that use Chinese characters.

16   Dilaçar, 163.

a systematic work in moral-political philosophy nor ethics; just as it is
neither a piece of poetry nor an allegoric story. Written mostly in dialogues, we can argue that *KB* is essentially a hermeneutical work that
situates and discusses the main principles of knowledge that lead to
happiness and justice. Accordingly, the fundamental issues relating to
human happiness and justice are thought by engaging with the meaning of poetic word which provides a sharper image of human existence.

The last section of *KB* where the author offers his apologies to the
reader is as follows:

6617. *Keyik tagı kördüm bu türkçe sözüg,*
        anı akru tuttum yakurdum ara

        I deemed this Turkish language like a deer
        I held it gently, brought closer to me

6618. *Sıkadım sevittim könül birdi terk,*
        takı ma belinler birerde yire

        As I caressed it, it loved me quickly
        Time to time it is in awe, bashfully

6619. *Sunup tutmışımça ederdim sözüg,*
        kelü berdi ötrü yıparı bura

        As I captured and rubbed the word
        Its musk happened upon me

6620. *Köni sözledim söz, irig hem açığ,*
        köni sözni yüdgen ukuşlug ere

        Truthfully I said it, thus hard and bitter
        Those who can bear the true word are wise

6621. *Okıglıka artuk ağır kelmesün,*
        özüm 'uzrı koldum aça hem yora

Upon reading it shall not be heavy
I offered my apologies, tried to explain and unravel it

6622. *Köni sözde taştın sözüg söz teme,*
köni egri farkı ürüŋli kara

Do not call it a word if it is not the true word
The difference between them is as white and black

6623. *Yıl altmış iki erdi tört yüz altmış iki bile,*
bu söz sözledim-men tutup cân süre

It was the year four hundred sixty-two
When I spoke these words in my lifetime

6624. *Tükel on sekiz ayda aydım bu söz,*
Ödürdüm, adırdım söz evdip tire

I spoke these words in eighteen months in total
I selected, distinguished and gathered them

6625. *Yadım tü çiçek teg yıdı kin burar,*
Ötündüm men, itnü tükettim, tura

I effused the words like flowers and musk
Forgive me for exhausting, here they remain

6626. *Sözüg kim tüketür neçe sözlese,*
aka tınmaz erter bulaklar ara

Who can exhaust the speech, no matter how much one speaks
it streams without ceasing between the sources.[17]

Before presenting my interpretation of these couplets, let me share some hermeneutical clarifications that can help identify my point of departure and the main point of focus at issue.[18] Hermeneutics intervenes when a text is deemed to be incomplete, posing difficul-

---

17 *KB*, 6617–6626: 651–652.
18 From a philological standpoint, my interpretation of Balasaguni's couplets will not offer much of a novelty. My aim remains limited to shedding light on a hermeneutic idea that strikes me, which I will explicate topologically: an experience of the inexhaustibility of meaningfulness places us in the between, that is, language as the undefinable, uncontrollable space of relationality.

ties for our understanding. A translation that interprets and an interpretation that interprets does not amount to building a mere bridge
between two language-worlds, as if two horizons of understanding
at stake are preestablished poles that can be immediately connected.
For that matter, the very place of the between that make spaces for a
possible connection must be experienced and inhabited. The departure point of any interpretation is the middle space of inter-connect-
edness, namely, the very condition of the possibility of any relationality. The interpretation of *KB* emerges out of that middle space in
the between, where middle Turkic, modern Turkish, and English are
placed in a hermeneutic dialogue. In this light, even though Turkish is my mother tongue, the interpretation at issue can be regarded
as an inter-cultural engagement. The idea of interculturality at issue
here does not denote a comparison of monolithic culture worlds.
The existence of any cultural whole is only possible on the grounds
of previous historical dialogues and connections, namely of "fusions
of horizons"[19] with other understandings of the world, which themselves are essentially pluralistic. What that also implies is that the
interpretation below focuses on the very place of language, which
is connected to the language of place insofar as the inter- of interculturality hints at the place of the between.[20] Although *KB* can be
read from so many perspectives, this is the topo-logical basis of my
approach that focuses on the place of saying which is equally a saying of place. In other words, Karakhanid Turkic is brought into the
neighborhood of English and Turkish as modern languages and we
look at its philosophical sense from the viewpoint of contemporary
philosophical problems.

The couplets that I have chosen to interpret are located at the final
section of the work, where we hear the poet's voice from his philosophical point of view, which can be considered a philosophical dialogue with his poetry. The first couplet is remarkable for underlining
the significance of writing his work in Turkic:

Keyik tagı kördüm bu türkçe sözüg,

---

19   Gadamer, 305.
20   Steven Burik, *The End of Comparative Philosophy and the Task of Comparative
     Thinking: Heidegger, Derrida and Daoism* (Albany: SUNY Press, 2009), 2.

anı akru tuttum yakurdum ara

I deemed this Turkish language like a deer
I held it gently, brought closer to me.[21]

In the historical context of 11th century, writing a work of poetry
in Turkic languages was undervalued in the wake of overwhelming
influence of Persian and Arabic, which were languages spoken and
written by the literary elites, statesmen and religious authorities. In
comparison with these languages, Turkic languages were considered
dull for various reasons: agglutinative languages offer relatively limited possibilities of end-rhymes due to the structure of suffixes[22]; they
comprise a strict vowel harmony, thus phonemes sound repetitive and
monotonous for the non-speakers.[23] In a way, Turkic languages were
considered the language of "barbarians" coming from the steppes of
Inner Asia. Against this background, we can understand why Balasaguni represents the Turkish language [*türkçe sözüg*] like a wild deer
[Karakhanid: *keyik*; Modern Turkish: *geyik*], which is shy, untamed,
and distant. "The language," or as *söz* can also connote, "the word"
needs to be approached gently and with attentiveness so as not to
be scared off, otherwise it can simply run away and disappear. The
language is "brought near" carefully; once it is caressed and shown
love, a bond is created between the poet and the word, or the Turkish
language.

Developing the poetic of image of deer, the couplets 6619 and
6620 offer an interesting passage that animates the essence of language as a scent:

---

21   *KB*, 6617: 651.

22   For example, Turkish *bilmiyorum* (I don't know): *bil* (know) + *m* (negative) +
     (i)-yor (present tense suffix) + (u)m (first person singular). Vowel harmony means,
     back (a, ı, o, u) or front vowels (e, i, ö, ü) follow the same type of vowels (Turkish:
     Gidemeyeceğim (I won't be able to go); *Bunu okumuştum* (I had read this).

23   In order to contest the negative impression of the Turkic languages, 11th century
     Karakhanid lexicographer Kaşgarlı Mahmut, meaning "Mahmut from the city
     of Kashgar" known also as Mahmut al-Kashgari, has written the most important
     scholarly work of lexicography of Turkic languages in Baghdad entitled *Diwan
     al Lughāt al-Turk* (*The Compendium of the dictionary of Turkic Languages*). The
     work is written bilingually in Karakhanid Turkic and Arabic, with the main aim of
     showing to the speakers of Arabic the richness and beauty of Turkic languages.

Sunup tutmışımça ederdim sözüg,
kelü berdi ötrü yıparı bura

As I captured and rubbed the word
Its musk happened upon me

As the poet embraces and firmly presses the language and its words against himself, the language releases its captivating musk (*yıpar*). This implies that the deer at issue, which is thought as the Turkish language, must be a musk deer. Indeed, what is poetically and philosophically noteworthy is the description of the essence of language literally as an *essence*. The poet's embrace of the deer frees the musk, which is the essence of the language of Turks. Earlier in *KB*, Balasaguni considers musk as knowledge that cannot be hidden. Knowledge, as the essence of language, is like an attractive scent which makes itself easily be identified even from afar.[24] At this point, the musk captures and mesmerizes the poet, which implicates a twofold movement of captivation: language captures us as we capture its words. The very idea of captivation, especially in regards with our relation to language is important, which reappears in a different manner only a few lines below. The couplets 6620–6624 express the core matter of the poet's apology, providing biographical information regarding the date of his poetry, elaborating how he managed to select and distinguish his words, until the couplet 6625 where the idea of the language as a scent and essence comes back into view. The couplets 6625 and 6626 constitute the most important part of this final section, which I will examine more closely.

As I have mentioned, *KB* devotes many sections to the relationship between knowledge, language and justice, especially in the seventh and nineteenth sections through a series of dialogues. For Balasaguni, the whole idea of writing this work of poetry emerges from and depends on the possibility of saying the true word (*köni söz*).[25] We can interpret this with a brief insight into Balasaguni's idea of the human being (*yalñguk*), which is issued in the couplet 197:

---

24   *KB*, 46: 312.
25   *KB*, 6620: 651.

bu yalñguk atı boldı yañgluk üçün
bu yañgluk uruldı bu yalñguk üçün

This name (the human being) has been given to the human being as (it)[26] errs
To err is created for the human being (the one who errs)[27]

The word's etymology literally means "the mistaken one" deriving from the verb *yanıl-*, thus *yañgluk* (to make a mistake), and the noun *yañ* (side, edge). What that means is the human being can lack the true word simply because the human being is designated as the kind of being that errs, makes mistakes, the one who can go astray and be wrong. As such, we are fundamentally hermeneutic beings who are prone to interpret things in the world. The human being either "teaches" (ögretigli) or "learns" (ögrenür), the third possibility is only the way of being of the beasts, specifically, randomly roaming horses (*yılkı*).[28] The human being is situated between the dialogue of teaching and learning, the former being a sign of wisdom, the latter being a sign of reason and understanding. Teaching and learning occurs through our following of the true word which aims for bringing righteousness and justice.

We can inquire: where is the origin from which the true and false word can emerge then? Indeed, Kün-toğdı asks his vizier Ay-toldı concerning the source of language:

kayudın çıkar söz kayuka barır
munı ma ayu bir manga ay bilir

From where does the word emerge, where does it arrive
Inform me on this, O the wise one[29]

Ay-toldı responds by saying that "the belonging place of language is secrecy, and one should keep one word out of ten to oneself."[30] This is in line with the overall idea that for Balasaguni the true wisdom of

---

26　Since in Turkish the personal pronouns he/she/it are the same (*o*), I choose to say "it" here.
27　*KB*, 197: 36.
28　*KB*, 3217: 327.
29　*KB*, 996: 117.
30　*KB*, 998: 117.

language depends on knowing when to speak and when to keep one's silence. The two-fold nature of language according to Balasaguni can also be exemplified in the couplet where language is designated as a "lion laying at the edge (*işik*/modern Turkish: *eşik*) of one's house, ready to eat one's head."[31] Language can bring good when the words are used warily, as much as it can bring evil if too much is said via idle-talk. The whole gist of language lies in being able to "untie thousands knots by saying only one word."[32] As Jean-Paul Roux remarks, Turkic languages allow for very long sentences in European languages to be expressed only in one word.[33] For that matter, Balasaguni's focus on reticence is important, which connects his thought with Asian perspectives on language.

Following that, the couplet that appears towards the end of Balasaguni's epilogue can be considered to capture the core matter of Balasaguni's account of language:

sözüg kim tüketür neçe sözlese
aka tınmaz erter bulaklar ara

who can exhaust the speech, no matter how much one speaks
it streams without ceasing between the sources[34]

Despite having treated language as a means of communication and a means to gain the true knowledge which will lead to justice, Balasaguni here designates language as a boundless phenomenon, a river that streams between the sources or springs beyond the control of the human being. This couplet is crucial considering the way in which it is connected to the previous couplet where Balasaguni writes:

Yadım tü çiçek teg yıdı kin burar,
Ötündüm men itnü tükettim, tura

I effused the words like flowers and musk
Forgive me for exhausting (them), here they remain[35]

---

31   *KB*, 164: 33.
32   *KB*, 172: 33.
33   Jean-Paul Roux, *Histoires des Turcs* (Paris: Fayard, 2000), 27.
34   *KB*, 6626: 652.
35   *KB*, 6625: 652.

Here, the idea of the language, and more specifically the idea of "the words" as the scent of musk (*kin*), appears again and is connected with the principal movement of language. At first, Balasaguni apologizes for exhausting the words, or the language. In a way, he signals that he has said too much and his poetry is about to come to an end. The word *tükettim* (I completed, ended, exhausted) can be interpreted both as "completing" and "bringing to completion." Now it is as if the flowers and the musk have no more fragrance left, which was the true essence of his poetic language. Nonetheless, this is why the following couplet cannot be separated from the preceding one: The poet can neither exhaust the language, nor the words. "It streams (*aka*) without ceasing (*tınmaz erter*) between (*ara*) the sources (*bulaklar*)."

What is hermeneutically interesting and worthy of question here is the manifold sense of the verb *tınmak*, meaning "taking a break, stopping, as well as breathing, inhaling"[36] in Karakhanid language. Modern Turkish verbs *dinmek* (coming to a standstill, stopping, slowing down) and *dinlemek* (listening, paying attention) seem to be connected to the root of the word *tın* signifying life, breath, soul.[37] In this regard, *tınmaz* (it does not cease—without breathing) hints at the possibility of a freer interpretation, even if only by its etymological associations and phonetic undertones. As such, to hear the manifoldness of meanings which are simply connoted by the phonetic proximity that *tınmaz* opens up, the line can be translated in a double sense:

sözüg kim tüketür neçe sözlese
aka tınmaz erter bulaklar ara

who can exhaust the language with abundance of words
it *breathlessly* streams between the sources

Linguistically, the modern Turkish equivalent of *tınmaz* would be *dinmez*, which could be used to describe the slowing down of a rainstorm while *dinlemez* would mean "s/he does not listen." As such, the very essence of the occurrence would imply a sense of restlessness that emerges from its ceaseless streaming. This hint should direct us to

---

36   Arat, *Kutadgu Bilig: İndeks III* (İstanbul: Edebiyat Fakültesi Basımevi, 1979), 442.
37   Clauson, 512.

the meaning of the source of language at issue. Language is streaming between the sources, and this act of streaming runs between the tranquillity of reticence and the disquiet of endlessness. As human beings, we are both exposed to the language's indifference to us, while we can also take part in its very streaming if we let ourselves and go adrift with it. In as much as we believe that we have exhausted the source from which language springs up and the essence which it releases, we are overwhelmed by its endless occurrence that quietens us.

Furthermore, considering the previous couplet, there is room also for the following interpretation: accordingly, language is not only a streaming water, but also the very air that we inhale. Poetic words are the scent of flowers and the fragrance of musk, which transpire when the occurrence of language is hearkened. If language and its words are to be thought as the streaming of a river between sources, this implicates that the event of language is both the place of happening and the happening of place. Situated between different cultural, religious and philosophical sources, the emergence of words themselves are both a quiet and disquieting happening that astonish us. Language is the taking place of the between.

3. *Towards a Dialogue Between Topology and Topographics of Language*

Although Balasaguni names language as a stream that runs "between the sources" (*bulaklar ara*), he does not delimit the boundaries of the sources. Does that mean that the language streams between the sources silently? What are these sources? Indeed, one is tempted to think that the language itself as a source. Nonetheless, language itself, although streaming, is situated between sources. That would mean that Balasaguni considers language as a river, running between the springs from which it arises and discharges into another body of water,[38] probably a lake or a sea. Yet, let us take a step back and con-

---

38   Gizem Z. Debreli's interesting work examines hydrographic words and concepts in Kaşgarlı Mahmut and Balasaguni's works. See Debreli, "Dîvânu Lugâti't-Türk ve Kutadgu Bilig'de Hidrografik Terimler ve Metaforik Kullanımları," *Ondokuz Mayıs Üniversitesi İnsan Bilimleri Dergisi (İBD)*, 1/2 (2020): 153.

sider the possibility that Balasaguni does not only mean to offer a metaphorical link between languages and rivers and consider the fact that he really aims to invite us to think the place-nature of language. In that sense, I would like to ask: what is the between (*ara*) as the between at issue?

Here I will try to make sense of the meaning of the between by putting his thought in a dialogue with Heidegger's later account of language, since Balasaguni's idea of the inexhaustible event of language shows certain similarities with Heidegger's critique of language as a means of communication and an organ of speech—especially with regards to the idea of topology and topographics of language as discussed in contemporary scholarship.[39] Let me state that my approach here is similar to the sort of philosophical comportment that Rorty holds towards Heidegger: Heidegger's philosophy is like a tool-box and we take what we consider to be a useful, and leave out what we find useless.[40] Balasaguni, as an 11th century Turkic-Muslim poet, has no immediate link to Heidegger's notion of being or language, as Heidegger has a philosophical agenda within the limits of modern Western thought.[41] In that sense, I am not arguing that there is a strong philosophical affinity between the two. However, I find it useful to point out that Balasaguni, despite belonging to what Heidegger would call a "metaphysical" way of thinking language,[42] was able to think the nature of language in a "non-metaphysical" manner.

---

39   See Krzysztof Ziarek, *Language after Heidegger*. Bloomington: Indiana University Press, 2013), 71; Malpas, *Heidegger's Topology: Being, Place, World* (Cambridge, Mass.: The MIT Press, 2006), 263. A more complete comparison could be offered between Balasaguni and Heidegger's interpretation of Hölderlin's hymn *The Ister* (Heidegger 1996), yet we leave this for another study that needs to focus on the possibility of a philosophical-poetic comparison between Balasaguni, Hölderlin, and Heidegger in more detail.

40   Richard Rorty, *Philosophy and Social Hope* (London: Penguin, 1999),191.

41   There are three footholds of Heidegger's intellectual trajectory: Phenomenologically, posing the question of the meaning–truth–place of being; historically, attempting to step into the boundaries of the overcoming of metaphysics; and politically stepping back from what he considers to be *das Gestell* as the essence of modern technology-Western *logos*.

42   Heidegger, *On the Way to Language*, 130. Heidegger likes to find a relationship between *dao* and the Alemannic–Swabian words *wëgen* and *be-wëgen*, which can be understood as the "way-making, clearing movement." The way-making movement (*Bewegung*) is key in understanding how Heidegger explains the topological

In criticizing the metaphysical notion of language that we find in European history of philosophy from Aristotle to Humboldt, Heidegger writes:

> Speaking implies that making of articulated sounds, whether we make them (in speaking), or refrain from making them (in silence), or are incapable of malting them (in loss of speech). Speaking implies the articulate vocal production of sound. Language manifests itself in speaking as the activation of the organs of speech-mouth, lips, teeth, tongue, larynx. The names by which language has called itself in the Western language, *glossa, lingua, langue,* language-are evidence that language has since ancient times been conceived in terms of these phenomena. Language is the tongue.[43]

Against this background, we can observe that Balasaguni's notion of language *til* (tongue), or *söz* (word) and *sözlemek* (the act of speaking, saying) is not different from the view that Heidegger considers to be the metaphysical understanding of language as self-expression, one that functions as a means of communication. For Heidegger, the word constitutes our linguistic relation to things, yet this does not mean that the word itself is only a linguistic component of the language. Insofar as the act of "saying" always discloses a certain aspect of the thing while concealing other meanings, at issue is the interplay between the "failure" (*Ver-sagen*) of the "saying" (*Sage*) of language. Here, the etymological relation between saying (*sagen*) and failure (*versagen*) comes to the fore, which links up with the idea of the stillness of language.

The stillness of language is an issue that is related to the notion of no-thingness, as the primary essence of being. Being (*Sein*) is not a thing, thus the question as to what being is can only make sense insofar as it is taken up with a focus on the concept of no-thingness. In *Being and Time,* Heidegger issues the same point that Balasaguni takes up in his poetry: the importance of stillness (*Stille*) as a way of evading idle-talk (*Gerede*) which is the inauthentic form of everyday discourse. As Kün-toğdı asks Ay-toldı why he is remaining silent,

---

connection between speaking, saying, and silence, as well as the relation between "words" (*Worte*) and "signs" (*Wörter*). For more on that topic, see Reinhard May, *Heidegger's Hidden Sources: East Asian Influences on His Work,* trans., Graham Parkes (London & New York: Routledge, 1996), 40.

43   Heidegger, *On the Way to Language,* 114.

Ay-toldı replies by saying that "what I am to say, as I have not been asked anything."[44] According to Ay-toldı, one who speaks without first being addressed must be considered a beast.[45] In response to this, confirming Ay-toldı is right in stating that, Kün-toğdı proffers that the human being is nevertheless bound to be a speaking being. If one does not speak at all, this is for two reasons: either one lacks knowledge and wisdom, or one is mute.[46] In Heidegger's case, instead of speaking at length or saying nothing, the authentic possibility of discourse lies in the capacity of hearkening to the silent speaking of the conscience, which says "no-thing."[47] Hearkening to the limits of discourse, instead of losing oneself in "idle-talk" (*Gerede*), indicates the possibility of the disclosure of human being's existence in its wholeness. It places one in the proper temporal direction of one's being-in-the-world, which is being-towards-death. This sense of nothingness can only be brought into language via the poetic word, for it can help us learn hearken to the stillness of saying.[48] Saying (*sagen*) is an astonishing action that calls for our philosophical sense of wonder in a different manner than the philosophers of language and linguists deal with language as an object of scientific inquiry. Here, it is interesting to note that from the word "saying" the adjective "legendary" (*Sagenhaft*) derives, which is also the root of the English word *saga*.[49] To that extent, what matters is not only what we say through language, but also arrive at a certain wisdom of language, where we experience how and why language fails and leaves us speechless.

One of the most important instances where Heidegger lays out his critique of the instrumentalist notion of language can be found in his interpretation of Stefan George's 1919 poem "The Word." Here Heidegger argues that a literary or philosophical clarification of the poem is not necessary for the saying of the poem, as if the poet's words are mere representations of sentiments that lack "argumenta-

---

44   *KB*, 957: 113.

45   *KB*, 962: 113.

46   *KB*, 969: 114.

47   Heidegger, *Being and Time*, 325.

48   For a detailed analysis of that topic, see the fourth section of my "Heidegger's Way to Poetic Dwelling via Being and Time," *Horizon: Studies in Phenomenology* 10:1 (2021), 268–285.

49   Heidegger, *On the Way to Language*, 93.

tive clarity." In doing so, "we would have reduced poetry to the servant's role as documentary proof for our thinking, and [...] in fact we
would already have forgotten the whole point: to undergo an experience with language."[50] Therefore, for Heidegger, the issue for the
philosopher is not the mere interpretation of the poem, but to con-
front the limitations of our interpretation. In that way, the poem can
be allowed its own hermeneutic space.[51] Here I will not cover Heidegger's analysis in its entirety, but only point towards a pertinent
matter that concerns Balasaguni's idea of language.

The last stanza of George's poem "The Word" reads as follows:

> *So lernt ich traurig den verzicht:*
> *Kein ding sei wo das wort gebricht.*

> So I renounced and sadly see:
> Where word breaks off no thing may be.[52]

Here, the colon that follows the word "see" initially suggests as
if the poet aims to provide an explanation. Grammarians call such
a mode of speech "direct discourse."[53] However, the next line of the
stanza does not provide a statement. This is because George does not
simply write "*ist*," but "*sei*." The colon appears as the "relation," that
is, "the between" that brings together the openness and boundedness
of language. This is where the movement between the thing and the
word takes place as the experience of language.[54] This is similar to the
relationship between the captivation of language and our captivation
by language. Balasaguni knows that as a poet he is bound to say the
word and exhaust the possibilities that language opens up for him. The
poetic line has been written and is put forward as if it were a "thesis."

---

50   Heidegger, *On the Way to Language*, 63.
51   Considering the link between the idea of the holiness and its relation the poetic
      word, Andrew Mitchell writes astutely: "the poetic word is born from a sacrifice of
      linguistic utility along with the relations that utility privileges and prescribes (clar-
      ity, univocity). As such, the word is allowed to resonate freely. The poetic word is
      released into its sounding. See, Andrew Mitchell, *The Fourfold: Reading the Late
      Heidegger* (Evanston: Northwestern University Press, 2016), 195–96.
52   Heidegger, *On the Way to Language*, 60.
53   Heidegger, *On the Way to Language*, 63.
54   Heidegger, *On the Way to Language*, 65.

Yet, Balasaguni is also aware that this is not the case. He can say the essence of language in an infinite number of ways and language would still be seeping through the existential hole which we as humans cannot fill. Language, as the running water or the air that fills our lungs is quietly continuing its own movement. In George's poem, the poet names the word, although this is not because a representation of the word lacks. The act of naming situates the human existence between the interplay of the world and its coming into meaningfulness. The space of "between" is marked with the colon. The placing of the colon does not permit us to read the poem only as an artistic object ready to be manipulated. The colon discloses the free space, or the between, that in which we are called to attend to the place of language.

It is against this background that Krzysztof Ziarek conceptualizes Heidegger's later thought of language under the title of topographics of language. Accordingly, the interval that exists between the word and the sign emerges from our incapacity to say the poetic word. Ziarek underscores that for Heidegger, the withdrawal of our experience of being comes to show itself through the failing nature of language. He argues, "When the word fails, when it does not reach dictionary words, that is, signs, the word, as it were, escapes and frees itself from signs. This escape marks the opening of the interval between signs and words, and as such it constitutes the hint of being."[55] The openness that is disclosed by the un-defined element of the "statement" is precisely what also de-limits and thus bounds them. In a certain sense, the colon functions as the in-bound of the two-way movement of the "thinking" and "poetizing" that is at issue, putting them into interplay, letting them entering into their respective fields by enveloping one another. In that context, Ziarek talks about the "dis-humanizing" (*Entmenschung*) effect of language. Human beings do not possess the language, but rather, they are "owned" (*eignet*) and "appropriated" (*geignet*); "attuned" (*stimmt*) and "determined" (*bestimmt*) by language. The "essential occurrence" of language is both its "failure" and "accomplishment" in the sense of its coming to completion and fullness.

---

55   Ziarek, 81.

In Balasaguni's work, the poetic experience of language remains within the topological space of meaning, without being topographically inscribed into the signs with which the betweenness of language can make itself be read. Even if Balasaguni had such intentions, we could not trace these signs since we do not have the original text and the archival state of the three existing copies of *KB* does not allow for such an investigation. Nonetheless, his designation of language as the happening of the between hints at such an experience of language.[56] The between (*ara*) as the free space of happening is also that which constitutes the places around itself. It brings them into a site of nearness of openness.

4. *The Limits of Asian Philosophy: From the Between*

Dealing with topology and topographics of language has shown why it is important to focus on the between. Here, let me shift the focus from the thinking of place to the place of thinking. I would like to ask two questions: (1) Where can we locate *KB*, written in a language that situates between East and West? (2) What are the philosophical implications of its situation for Asian philosophical texts? Looking into the place of *KB* opens up to discussion the very limits of Asian philosophies, just as well it urges us to ask the very meaning of betweenness at issue.

KB is the first Islamic work in Turkic literatures. One question that arises is whether it would not be more accurate to locate Balasaguni's work within the context of Islamic philosophy. Historically, Islam appears in the Arabic peninsula in the 7th century, situated in Southwestern or West Asia, in a region that is considered to be the opposite end of what corresponds to our commonplace image of Asia. Indeed, many scholarly works mention Turkic languages and Turkic intellec-

---

56 Readers of Turkish language can find a topographic mode of thinking in the writings of 20th century philosopher-poet Oruç Aruoba (1948–2020). For instance, a detailed study of Aruoba's *Kesik Esintiler* (1994), keeping contemporary French and German philosophy, as well as Aruoba's translation of Bashō's haikus in the hindsight, could show how Aruoba's topographics of language opens up unexplored possibilities of writing in modern Turkish language.

tual heritage only under the label of Islamic philosophy, referring to Turks within the greater Asian context mainly in terms of invasions.[57] More recently Raud whose very important work promises to cover all Asian worldviews and religions "throughout history," considers Islamic philosophy to belong to the Western intellectual tradition due to its connection to Abrahamic-monotheistic religions of Near East.[58] As such, Central Asia is excluded from the rest of the continent once again.

We can argue that more commonly known Asian traditions of thought such as Indic, Chinese, Korean, and Japanese philosophies produced many important philosophical works over the centuries, which is owing to their critical engagement with different religious-spiritual belief systems such as Hinduism, various forms of Buddhism, Shinto religion among other local religions. Comparably, *KB* was written in an age and geography where Islam was gradually becoming the chief religion among the Turkic peoples. Yet that does not mean that it belongs *only* to Islamic philosophy, especially if Islam is considered as a religion that belongs to Middle East as a region cut off from Asia. What is also problematic is that the limits of the so-called Middle East itself remain blurry and can change from one definition to another depending on one's geopolitical stance. Therefore, even the margins of Islamic philosophy need to be reexamined. Furthermore, the very limits of Islamic philosophy exceed the boundaries of West Asia and Islamic religion, since how Islam is practiced in Central Asia (mostly based on local Shamanistic religions) differs significantly from how it is practiced in the Arab world for historical and cultural reasons. While it is true that Islamic philosophy developed mostly on the basis of Plato and Aristotle's thought as well as Neo-Platonist thought, there are others who suggest that Islamic philosophy also came in close contact with East Asian belief systems and philosophies.[59]

---

57 Brian Carr and Indra Mahalingam, eds., *Companion Encyclopedia of Asian Philosophy* (London & New York: Routledge, 2005).

58 Rein Raud, *Asian Worldviews: Religions, Philosophies, Political Theories* (Hoboken, NJ: Wiley-Blackwell, 2021), vii.

59 Reza Shah et al., *Common Ground between Islam and Buddhism* (Fons Vitae: Loiseville, 2010), xvi.

Yet, the issue is not solely the place of Islamic philosophy. In Transoxiana region, Islam mostly replaced other religions such as Buddhism, Manicheism, Tengrism and Shamanism, that were being practiced by Turkic peoples up until the 11th century,[60] not to mention the known presence of Zoroastrianism, Nestorian Christianity, and other religions in and around the cities and areas where Turks lived.[61] The region from which *KB* emerges is an important Central Asian hub with profound historical and spiritual connections to Islam, but also to Buddhism and Western metaphysics. Far from being a reiteration of a religious worldview, and as a philosophical reengagement with basic political and ethical questions in human life, *KB* is an expression of a life-world that situates in the center of centuries-long philosophical and religious dialogues. In that light, viewing religion as a static cultural entity that can define the whole of a geographical region is a problematic point of view. In addition, why and how Mongolic tradition, which is a non-Islamic culture, is often separated from East Asia is also questionable.[62]

Here we are entitled to ask: where is Asia located? How and where should we locate it? Of course, this depends on where we are and from which perspective we are looking at the issue. *Asia* is originally an Akkadian word, deriving from the verb *asu* that designated the "region of the rising Sun."[63] However, at the time Asia referred not to the whole of the continent of Asia as we think of it today, but rather only to a region in the Westernmost region of Minor Asia. The historical region of *Anatolia*, which is the homeland of Turkish people since the 11th century, was the first concept of the West in the history of the West. Interestingly, the word Anatolia itself (ἀνατολή), which simply means "orient" in the Greek language, follows the same

---

60   Beckwith, 115.

61   Roux, 148–9.

62   For instance, today the role and place of Buddhism for early Turkic peoples in Central Asia is an ongoing discussion, which point towards the necessity a more comprehensive approach regarding the question of religion See Hans-Joachim Klimkeit, "Buddhism in Turkish Central Asia," *Numen*, 1990 (37) 1: 53–69; Jes P. Laut, *Der frühe türkische Buddhismus und seine literarischen Denkmäler: Veröffentlichungen der Societas Uralo-Altaica* (Wiesbaden: Harrassowitz, 1986).

63   Ernest Klein, *Klein's Comprehensive Etymology Dictionary of the English Language* (Elsevier: Amsterdam, 1971), 54.

etymological connection that we observe in the words *asu* and *Asia* in Akkadian. What that implies is that every geographical location, insofar as considered to be located in the "between" by its dwellers, may have its own "Asia" and "Europe" antagonism—the latter meaning the "land of the setting Sun" as the "Occident." Thinking the between and thinking from the between, however, requires us to see also the whole, and not only the margins.

Today we tend to consider vast regions that encompass countries such as India, China, Japan as indivisible wholes that exist as independent entities in themselves. This view does not only underestimate the fact that, just as anywhere in the world, peoples and languages of Asia influenced one another in a fundamental way, but it rests grounded in a geopolitical separation of places in terms of various factors such as statehood and religion. An inclination towards political-linguistic classification of places by all-encompassing names is partially related to the kind of Orientalism that emerged during the Occidental colonization of some parts of the Asian continent, which continues to determine the contours of our imagination of and intellectual interest in Asia. Yet, Western colonialism did not think in terms of neighborhoods, but regions and territories divisible in terms of material resources, races, ethnicities, tribes, sects and such.

In a certain way, other than being a mere bridge between the two already established ends such as Europe and Fareast, Central Asia can be seen as a region of neighborhood, a hermeneutic between out of which the very idea of Asia as a continental whole occurred. This is why it is important to get rid of the idea of the in-betweenness of Central Asia and reestablish the betweenness at issue in a hermeneutic way, that is, by engaging with the interpretation of texts from Central Asian region.

Only looking at a map of the Xiongnu as part of the *Wu Hu* from the 4th century, studying western and eastern borders of Göktürk Khanate from the 6th century, dealing with the question of religion in Uyghur Khanate from the 8–9th centuries, reading about the establishment of Yuan Dynasty in China by Kublai Khan in the 13–14th centuries, reviewing the formation of Mughal Empire in the Indian subcontinent by Babur in the 16th century, can already indicate to what extent the exchange and intermingling of cultures (which obviously was not always in peaceful terms), languages, religions, state-crafts, traditions, oral traditions have been not only influential, but central to the historical development and formation of Asia as a place. Historically, we observe that various nomadic, semi-nomadic and sedentary cultures of the Central Asian region from antiquity to modern ages were vital in making possible the trade routes between East Asia, Middle East and Europe. What is important to note is not only that this movement contributed to the exchange of ideas, scientific inventions, art techniques and such,[64] but it was precisely the reason of being of these intellectual human products themselves.

In concluding, I can perhaps try to respond to Beckwith's historical question that I have cited at the very outset of my article: we do not know what happened to all the "barbarians," because we did not sufficiently study the places that they inhabited, just as we did not try to understand what it means to be in the between. Beckwith's historical analysis shows to what extent the idea of "barbarians," a derogatory notion that developed in antiquity to designate Eurasian nomadic peoples, is a Eurocentric Greco-Roman fallacy.[65] In philosophy, most famously—and perhaps most unfortunately—Kant represented nomads and nomadic peoples as the destructors of civilization. In the preface of *Critique of Pure Reason*, Kant writes that those "barbarians," namely nomads who "loathe all steady cultivation of the soil, tore up from time to time the civil society" was luckily "few in number," thus the destruction that they could cause were relativized thanks to the foundationalist efforts of dogmatists.[66] Kant's association of nomadic peoples with sceptics, who, along with dogmatists and indifferentists, treated metaphysics ("the queen of all sciences") with despise to cast her out, is revelatory of a historically ignorant reflection based on wrong stereotypes, instead of historical literacy, or rational thinking, as one would expect from Kant. Although Bala-

---

64   Bruce E. Brooks traces the possibility of Chinese borrowing of certain philosophical ideas from Greeks. See his "Alexandrian Motifs in Chinese Texts," *Sino-Platonic Papers*, No. 96. As for the influence of Greek philosophy on Islamic thought, Majid's article offers a comprehensive historical account. See, Fakhry Majid, *Greek philosophy: impact on Islamic philosophy*, 1998, Routledge Encyclopedia of Philosophy, Taylor and Francis: doi:10.4324/9780415249126-H011-1

65   Beckwith, 321–22.

66   Kant, *The Critique of Pure Reason*, Aix–Ax.

saguni was not a nomad himself, given the cultural background and historical development of Turkic civilization in which he was brought up, he can easily qualify as a "barbarian." In the wake of geopolitical events of the last two centuries, Turkic cultures find themselves stuck in-between different political centers of dominance, such as Europe, Russia, Middle East and China. Nonetheless, if this situation of in-betweenness is reinterpreted from a topological standpoint, it shall open up fresh horizons of thought and help us make sense of herme-neutic neighborhoods of Asian philosophies from new perspectives.

References

Arat, R. Reşid, *Kutadgu Bilig:* İndeks III. İstanbul: Edebiyat Fakültesi Basımevi, 1979.

_____. *Kutadgu Bilig:* Metin I. İstanbul: Milli Eğitim Basımevi, 1947.

Aruoba, Oruç. *Kesik Esintiler.* İstanbul: Mephisto Yayınevi, 1994.

Beckwith, I. Christopher. 2009. *Empires of the Silk Road: A History of Central Eurasia from the Bronze Age to the Present.* Princeton and Oxford: Princeton University Press.

Brooks, E. Bruce. 1999. *Alexandrian Motifs in Chinese Texts. Sino- Platonic Papers,* No. 96. Philadelphia: University of Pennsylvania.

Burik, Steven. *The End of Comparative Philosophy and the Task of Comparative Thinking: Heidegger, Derrida and Daoism.* Albany: SUNY Press, 2009.

Clauson, Gerard. *An Etymological Dictionary of Pre-Thirteenth-Century Turkish.* Oxford: Oxford University Press, 1972.

Carr, Brian, and Mahalingam, Indira (ed.) *Companion Encyclopedia of Asian Philosophy.* London & New York: Routledge, 2005.

Dankoff, Robert. *Wisdom of Royal Glory (Kutadgu Bilig): A Turko-Islamic Mirror for Princes by Yusuf Khass Hajib.* Translated with an introduction and notes by Robert Dankoff. Chicago and London: The University of Chicago Press, 1983.

_____. *From Mahmud Kaşgari to Evliya Çelebi.* Piscataway, NJ: Gorgias Press, 2009.

Debreli, Z. Gizem. *Dîvânu Lugâti't-Türk ve Kutadgu Bilig'de Hidrografik Terimler ve Metaforik Kullanımları.* Ondokuz Mayıs Üniversitesi İnsan Bilimleri Dergisi (İBD), 1/2, Aralık / December 2020, 139–167.

Dilaçar, Agop. *Kutadgu Bilig İncelemesi.* Ankara: Türk Dil Kurumu Yayınları, 1995.

Fakhry, Majid. *Greek philosophy: impact on Islamic philosophy*, 1998, doi:10.4324/9780415249126-H011-1. Routledge Encyclopedia of Philosophy, Taylor and Francis.

Gadamer, Hans-Georg. *Truth and Method*. Translated by Joel Weinsheimer and Donald G. Marshall. London and New York: Continuum, 2004.

Heidegger, Martin. *On the Way to Language*. Translated by P. D. Hertz. New York: Harper & Row Publishers, 1971.

_____. *Being and Time*. Translated by J. Macquarrie and E. Robinson. Oxford: Blackwell Publishing, 1985.

_____. *Hölderlin's Hymn: The Ister*. Translated by W. McNeill and J. Davis. Bloomington: Indiana University Press, 1996.

Jamal, Gulnisa, Kafkasyalı S. Muhammet. (eds). *Kutadgu Bilig Araştırmaları Tarihi*. Ankara: Karınca Yayınları, 2016.

Karamercan, Onur. *Heidegger's Way to Poetic Dwelling via Being and Time*. Horizon: Studies in Phenomenology 10 (2021): 268–285.

Kant, Immanuel. *The Critique of Pure Reason*. Translated by M. Gregor. Cambridge: Cambridge Universe Press, 2015.

Kazemi, Reza Shah et al. *Common Ground between Islam and Buddhism*. Louisville, KY: Fons Vitae, 2010.

Klein, Ernest. *Klein's Comprehensive Etymology Dictionary of the English Language*. Elsevier: Amsterdam, 1971.

Klimkeit, Hans-Joachim. *Buddhism in Turkish Central Asia*. Numen, 37 (1990): 53–69.

Laut, P. Jens. *Der frühe türkische Buddhismus und seine literarischen Denkmäler*. *Veröffentlichungen der Societas Uralo-Altaica*. Harrassowitz, Wiesbaden, 1986.

Malpas, Jeff. *Heidegger's Topology: Being, Place, World*. Cambridge, Mass.: The MIT Press, 2006.

_____. *Heidegger and the Thinking of Place: Explorations in the Topology of Being*. Cambridge, MA: The MIT Press, 2012.

May, Reinhard. *Heidegger's Hidden Sources: East Asian Influences on His Work*. Trans. Graham Parkes. London & New York: Routledge, 1996.

Mitchell, Andrew. *The Fourfold: Reading the Late Heidegger*. Evanston: Northwestern University Press, 2015.

Raud, Rein. *Asian Worldviews: Religions, Philosophies, Political Theories*. Hoboken, NJ: Wiley-Blackwell, 2021.

Rorty, Richard. *Philosophy and social hope*. London: Penguin, 1999.

Roux, Jean-Paul. *Histoires des Turcs*. Paris: Fayard, 2000.

Savelyev, Alexander, and Robbeets, Martine. *Bayesian phylolinguistics infers the internal structure and the time-depth of the Turkic language family*. *Journal of Language Evolution*, 5 (2020): 39–53. https://doi.org/10.1093/jole/lzz010

Ziarek, Krzysztof. *Language after Heidegger.* Bloomington: Indiana University Press, 2013.

Žižek, Slavoj. "Language, Violence and non-Violence." *International Journal of Zizek Studies*, 2: 3 (2008): 1–12.

TRANSLATIONS

Diana Yüksel (University of Bucharest)

MEWŎLDANGMUNJIP
BOOK 16, "MISCELLANEOUS"

Introduction

Poet, philosopher, fiction writer, Confucian scholar and devout Buddhist, Kim Sisŭp 金時習 (1435–1493), pen-name Mewŏldang (梅月堂), is one of the most enigmatic Korean writers of the fifteenth century. A promising Confucian prodigy, Kim Sisŭp had shocked the society of his time by retiring from the public life and becoming a Buddhist monk in 1455 as a form of protest after King Sejo (r. 1455–1468) usurped of the throne from his nephew, King Tanjong (r. 1452–1455).

Kim Sisŭp is best known for his collection of short stories *The New Tales of the Golden Turtle Mountain* (*Kŭmo sinhwa* 金鰲新話), which is but a figment of his enormous volume of work, consisting of twenty three volumes in *The Complete Works of Mewŏldang* (*Mewŏldangmunjip* 梅月堂文集) and many other texts that are kept in Buddhist sources. One of the most prolific writers of the fifteenth century, Kim Sisŭp left behind an impressive number of poems of Confucian, Buddhist and Daoist inspiration, various Confucian-themed essays, Buddhist commentaries on Zen and Huayan treatises and fictional stories. His work appears to be eclectic, but it is consistent, converging towards formulating a moral philosophy, centered around the idea of righteousness and just conduct (*ŭiri* 義理), regardless of the doctrinarian affiliation.

The three chapters translated here are form the sixteenth volume of the complete works, which consists of ten essays debating key concepts in East-Asian philosophy from a triple perspective—Confucian, Buddhist and Daoist, hence it is titled *Miscellaneous* (*Chapch'e* 雜著). The selected fragments are a sample of Kim Sisŭp's vast knowledge of Confucian classics, but also his insight into Buddhist and Daoist teachings as well as his flexible attitude towards all thought forms.

1. *Without thoughts* (Musa 無思 第一)

Ch' ŏng Hancha said:

"In the old days, people practiced the Way (Dao) and treasured each moment of their time. They never abandoned their ways, nor did they feel complacent. People of our times have no thoughts and no concerns all day long. When will they thoroughly realize that?"

A visitor then contradicted him:

"By nature, the Way is without thoughts and without concerns.[1] Therefore, the thoughts and worries are but delusions. How could one follow the Way with thoughts and anxiety?"

Ch' ŏng Hancha replied:

"The essence of the Way is having no arbitrary thoughts and no anxiety and it is important to achieve this by thinking thoroughly and not letting oneself be neglectful. To always look at the things of the world, but to never have a worry, is letting all things break into pieces like fragile roof tiles. How then could such a person grasp the perfect and flawless Way? In the past, Ji Wen Zi had thought three times before acting once, the Master [Confucius] had set nine things to be considered when acting,[2] and Zeng Zi, thinking thoroughly, recorded the Master's teachings. The Master warned that one should think ahead, cultivate one's nature earnestly and strengthen one's will without waiting in vain. How then can one be without thoughts?

---

1   The argument here begins from the spontaneity of *Dao*, a trait emphasized equally by Confucian, Buddhist and Daoist traditions. In *The Daodejing*, Chapter two, it is said "The Way is like an empty vessel" 道沖而用之或不盈.

2   Reference to the following passage from *The Analects* (16.10.): "The exemplary man gives thought to nine things: in looking he should see clearly; in hearing he should use his wisdom; in his appearance he should be cordial; in his deeds he should be reverent; in his speech he should be honest, in conducting his affairs he should be respectful, in doubting he should think about asking questions, in envisioning benefits he should think about righteousness." 孔子曰: 君子有九思：視思明，聽思聰，色思溫，貌思恭，言思忠，事思敬，疑思問，忿思難，見得思義.

People's dispositions are all different, in the same way that there is darkness and brightness, foolishness and wisdom. How can one acquire sagehood without being assiduous and constant? Surely then, only after one has cultivated himself and straightened up one's thoughts, practiced [the Way] every day and polished [his nature] every month, can one say in true awareness that the Way is without thoughts and without worry."

The visitor then said:

"The teachings of our society (*pangnae* 方內) bring forth the rule of the Rites (*ye* 禮) and make clear from the beginning to the end[3] the [importance of the] Three Fundamental Bonds,[4] the Five Constant Virtues,[5] the Eight Stages[6] and the Nine Canons.[7] The learn-

---

3   Allusion to the first chapter of the Confucian classic *The Great Learning* (*Daxue* 大學): "All things have their roots and branches, all affairs have their ends and beginnings. To know what comes first and what comes after is to be near the Dao" 物有本末, 事有終始, 知所先後, 則近道矣.

4   *Samgang* 三綱 (Ch. *San gang*), Three Fundamental Bonds is one of the core Confucian terms, referring to the basic relationships that form the foundation of the society: the relationship between the ruler and his subjects, the relationship between the father and son and that between husband and wife. The concept is present all along the history of Confucianism, but it became more prominent during Song dynasty in China, with the rise of the new Confucian theories.

5   *Osang* 五常 or *Oryun* 五倫 (Ch. *Wu chang* or *Wu lun*) refers to the Five Constant Virtues, a concept that together with that of the Three Fundamental Bonds define the most important human relations and social virtues. Following the rule of the Five Constant virtues, the relationship between father and son should be governed by affection (*pujayuch'in* 父子有親), the relationship between ruler and subject should be governed by righteousness (*kunshinyuŭi* 君臣有義), the relationship between husband and wife should abide by their different roles (*pubuyubyŏl* 夫婦有別), the relationship between senior and young should be based on hierarchical order (*changyuyusŏ* 長幼有序), the relationship between friends should rely on trustworthiness (*punguyushin* 朋友有信).

6   The Eight Stages (*palcho*; Kr., *ba tiao*; Ch. 八條) are steps on the path of self-cultivation, explained in *The Great Learning*, which should be followed in order: (1) Investigating things (*kyŏngmul* 格物); (2) Extending knowledge (*ch'iji* 致知); (3) Making intentions genuine (*sŏngŭi* 誠意); (4) Balancing the mind (*chŏngshim* 正心); (5) Refining one's person (*sushin* 修身); (6) Aligning one's household (*chega* 齊家); (7) Ordering the state (*ch'iguk* 治國); (8) Setting the world at peace (*p'yŏngch'ŏnha* 平天下).

7   *Kugyŏng* 九經 (Chinese: *Jiu jing*) is found in the Confucian classic *The Doctrine of the Mean* (*Zhongyong* 中庸) and refers to the The Nine Moral Principles or the Nine Canons that form the basis of government: (1) refine one's person (*sushin* 修身); (2) honor the worthy (*chonhyŏn* 尊賢), (3) keep to one's kin (*ch'inch'in* 親親),

ing follows a hierarchical order from the master to the disciples, from the investigation of things (*kyŏngmul* 格物) to the restauration of the peace (*p'yŏngch'ŏnha* 平天下),[8] from the ruler down to his people.[9] To finish one thing today and then another thing tomorrow, to acquire the daily habit and the monthly cultivation of the self is the way of the sage. Thus, *The Book of Changes* speaks thoroughly and with admiration about these principles and records the words of the sages that talk about the effort of carefully considering and clearly distinguishing [between things], so that things in the world follow their meaningful way and there is no disorder and, while living in the same world, [the sage] is clearly distinct from other creatures such as birds and beasts or barbarians. If we talk of a scholar retreated from society (*panwoe* 方外) who sits in meditation having detached himself from the world, all his thoughts are peaceful, he does not have to bow to the lords and the rulers, he does not have to show mindfulness towards his relatives, therefore he can happily and open-heartedly turn (*kwi* 歸) towards embracing a life that is shared with the birds and the beasts, since there is no place that he would set his heart to and he would not be bothered by thoughts and worries."

Ch'ŏng Hancha said:

"Is a hermit truly unconcerned about things? If one does not tend to reach one's utmost, is that an absence of thoughts? Usually, for the people of the world to meditate (*sŏn* 禪) means to contemplate in a state of peacefulness, but one cannot know that *sŏn* means necessarily to cultivate oneself and to think quietly. Between Heaven and earth,

---

(4) respect high ministers (*kyŏngdaeshin* 敬大臣); (5) empathize with all officers (*ch'egunshin* 體群臣); (6) treat the common people as your children (*chasŏmin* 子庶民); (7) attract the skilled craftsmen (*naebaekkong* 來百工); (8) treat those distant from you with gentleness (*yuwŏnin* 柔遠人); (9) cherish the patrician lords (*hoejehu* 懷諸侯). Cf. *The Doctrine of the Mean*, Section IV.b., based on the translation by A. Charles Muller.

8   Paraphrase of the principles stated in *The Great Learning* and *The Doctrine of the Mean* that in order to rule the country or the world correctly, one must start from setting one's own body and mind-heart in order, then establishing the order in one's own family, then in one's community and then in the country.

9   Another allusion to the first chapter from *The Great Learning*: "From the Son of Heaven to the common person, for all alike, refining the person is the root" 自天子 以至於庶人，壹是皆以修身爲本.

humans are the most brilliant and their wisdom is the highest among the myriad things. Even if the obvious and the hidden are differentiated, how can one not learn something for a day or not think for a day? Obviously, learning without thinking is impossible and thinking without learning is perilous,[10] therefore thinking does not mean to harbor evil thoughts, but [only] to consider the meaning of the Way. Contemplating does not mean to fall into madness, but only to reflect on what has been learned. When walking in the front yard of a house or strolling about in the fields, the eyes see and the mind-heart reflects. This is a natural way of cultivating oneself, therefore one can never give up learning. That is why, when climbing a mountain, one considers learning about reaching high, when looking down at the water, one considers learning about profundity, when sitting on a rock, one considers learning about firmness, when admiring a pine tree, one considers learning about rectitude, when gazing at the moon, one considers learning about brightness. The shape of the myriad things appears in the tiny space of the bright mind-heart and since each of these things has its own virtues, we must learn about them and, by investigating thoroughly, we can decipher their mystery and enter the realm of sages. [Even so] I cannot know the utmost extent of the Way."

2. *The woods* (Sanrim 山林 第二)

Ch' ŏng Hancha said:
"People of the ancient times lived in the woods and fed themselves with what was found on the hills and in the valleys, and they would diligently use the compasses and the ruler,[11] become renowned teachers and through their deeds, they would perpetuate the long-lasting Way. But nowadays, even if they clean their houses

---

10   Reference to Confucius, *The Analects* (2.15): "The Master said, "Learning without thought leads to loss; thought without learning leads to danger" 子曰: 學而不思則 罔, 思而不學則殆.

11   *Kyuku* (規矩) is a term detached from a phrase in *The Book of Rites* (*Liji* 禮記), which says "To measure things with the compasses and the ruler" that is meant to say "To judge things according to a set of rules and standards".

and brighten them up and keep their places warm and tidy, they are still affected by laziness and negligence. How then could they cultivate themselves?"

A visitor again contradicted him:

"The compasses and the ruler and the norms of conduct are the [essence of the] perpetual law of the world. The freedom and openness are the [essence of the] law of nature. When one can drink the water from the mountain brooks, feed oneself with pigweed and rest one's body in a quiet place, what need is there for compasses and ruler?"

Ch'ŏng Hancha smiled and asked:

"What are these 'compasses and ruler' that we are talking about?"

The visitor answered:

"They are formal standards (*pŏpto* 法度)."

Ch'ŏng Hancha asked again:

"And what are formal standards?"

The visitor said:

"One's attire should be orderly, one's attitude dignified. When handling a cup of water full to the brim, one should hold it [with care] as if holding a piece of jade. One should show dignity even in front of fear; this is called nobleness. One should emulate good manners; this is called demeanor. But what need does a scholar living in the woods, whose worn-out hemp clothes barely cover his limbs and his tilted hood barely reaches to his ears, have to put on the dignitary belt and assume a distinguished air in his manner of clothing and of his speech? Moreover, if the deer and stags, fish and birds are not creatures of reason and manner and the high rocks and the deep pits are not the places where one would stroll about with elegance, then where would one carry out the formal standards that we are talking about?"

Ch'ŏng Hancha laughed out loud and said:

"I see that you only know the norms and standards of our society, but you are not aware of the rules and the precepts that transcend our world. I shall teach you. The Way has no beginning and no end and its rule cannot be expressed in words, so if you think that the rules of conduct apply only to the way you adorn your body, then you are one who does not understand the fundamental principles.

What the scholar follows is the Way, what he grasps is the meaning. When one follows the Way, even in the absence of clothes and ornaments, he is still dignified, when one grasps the meaning he can justly judge things even in the absence of standards. Master Confucius commended the virtue of covering one's head and donning the official attire, otherwise how could one recognize a general or a minister when they swung their swords or fed their cattle, so that someone like Duke Huan of Qi[12] could appoint them as councilors to the throne? This is what the formal standards are about. The scholar who has retreated from the world cannot be committed to following the Way and if he cannot set its meaning firmly, he could lose his life to starvation or weariness,[13] his existence could be wrecked by hardships and persecutions. Then how could one say that drinking the water from the stream is better than being summoned by the monarch three times and eating wild roots is satisfying for the rest of one's life? Surely even if one's food is made of mixed grains and vegetables, one can be broad-minded and generous. Even if one's sitting place is made from shrubs and his gate from thorns, one can clearly understand the meaning [of things], and replicate [the morals from] the times of the emperors Yao and Shun, his wide gaze encompasses both past and present, he can follow the natural flow of things and find his peace and calm in non-action. Even if his body does not abide by the formal standards, his intentions are clear for the others, and even if he cannot distinguish between grass

---

12   Qi Huan Gong (濟桓公), ruler of the State of Qi during the Spring and Autumn period, known also as the "Age of Hegemons", a time of struggle for power between rival states. Duke Huan was renowned for his capable advisors, one of them being the philosopher Guan Zhong (管仲), author of the earliest political and philosophical texts, the *Guanzi* compilation. Together, they reformed the State of Qi, making it one of the most powerful. As a result, Duke of Huan became the most prominent of the Five Hegemeons (*Wu Ba* 五霸), extremely powerful rulers of the era.

13   Reference to the "Story of Bo Yi (伯夷) and Shu Qi (叔齊)", first recorded in the *Book of History* (*Shiji* 史記), also known as *Records of the Grand Historian*, by Sima Qian (司馬遷, 145-86 BCE). Sons of the ruler of Guzhu State, towards the end of the Shang Dynasty, around the first millennium BCE, Bo Yi and Shu Qi remained in history as emblems of morality. Standing firm by their principles, they refused to eat any crops that grew on the land of King Wu, and fed themselves with roots and ferns, which led to their death by starvation.

and trees, he earns the reverence of the myriad things, the fish and birds and monkeys are touched by his virtue and the people and the Heaven cherish his Way. These are the grounds on which the masters of the eternal Way were established."

The visitor then said:

"The scholar who follows the Way stays in the woods and forgets about the world, his mind-heart is not corrupted by the profit and his virtue does not succumb to any temptation. Isn't it right to say that this is the true master of the eternal Way?"

Ch' ŏng Hancha said:

"Your words are beautiful, no doubt, but the ones who truly master the Way do not know that they follow the Way. Not all people who master the Way have a wish to retreat to the woods and not all who follow the Way in the world are willing to make it obvious. If they want to act [according to the Way] they act and if they want to leave everything, they do so. Then there are those who go far away and cry every time they bake their taro roots, and those who are willingly coming down from the mountains dragging their walking sticks. When times are turning, their acts are not contrary to the Way, when the sincerity prevails, their words are not spoken against the changes. Since they do not seek profit, their words can be straightforward and honest, since they do not care for fame, their deeds are correct and austere, since they do not run away from poverty, their words are deeply moving the kings and monarchs, since they do not fear death, their guiding principles make them fully aware of this insignificant world of ours. There are monarchs who practice the rites (*ye* 禮) and reverence (*kŏng* 敬), and yet not reach high, and [there are those who] can join the palanquin bearers and yet not fall low. Even with many words of defamation, their Way goes stronger. Even when attacked in treacherous ways, their teachings do not perish. If there is a scholar whose Virtue is like this, then he truly is the master of the eternal Way. Therefore it is useless to compare such a person who is filled with morality (*todŏk* 道德) with one who praises himself, places himself above others and seeks only profit and fame."

3. *Royal summoning (Samch'ŏng* 三請 第三*)*

A visitor said:

"In the old days, there was a revered master[14] who received the royal summoning three times, but did not go [to the palace] and his shadow never left the mountain. Surely he did not bother reforming the myriad things[15] and only cared for cultivating himself. At the same time, there are in our world scholars who live in the countryside, farming or doing public works, who answered after they received the royal call three times, and some even answered after they were called only once. This was done for the sake of following the Way, for the people, for aiming to [help the monarch] be morally accomplished like emperors Yao and Shun. The scholars who live among others would rather do the same. How can we then truly say that the above person is a revered master? If one listens to the wise men this is "to protect only one's treasure and forsake one's country", a denunciation that cannot be neglected. Then how [are we to understand this]?"

Ch'ŏng Hancha replied:

"Why should we talk about this in such inflexible words? The Buddhist *Dharma* is clear and pure and free of greed. To say that for the one in the woods, to not care for the myriad things, means to dedicate himself to the Way, and for the one among the people means to practice his virtue is very stern. Even if the world is corrupt and people do not follow the moral law,[16] it is possible to have no worry and live peacefully, [just as well as] in a world where the Way is practiced there can be a lack of happiness (*pi ka hwan* 非可歡). If to practice the Way means to live in poverty on mountains and in the fields one should still find joy [in it], to follow the *Dharma* in society means that even when discussing the scriptures with the monarch one should not be arrogant. To enjoy a peaceful, bountiful life, to have no restrictions and no restrains, this is a great Buddhist master's way.[17] For the virtuous Confucian scholar, this is not the way, for he studied since childhood and grew up practicing the norms. [Therefore] in times of

---

14   In the text, *kosŭng* 高僧, a monk of high virtue and learning, a Buddhist high priest.

15   In original *mul* 物, but most likely a substitution for "all things" (*manmul* 萬物).

16   Buddhist *Dharma*.

17   In original "advance and retreat" (*kŏch'wi* 去就), meaning "one's course of action".

misfortune, when the world is in chaos and when times are dangerous and the monarch is sending admonitions, he does not respond. Some scholars prefer to go fishing in the North Sea,[18] others just hang their hats at the East Gate (*Tongmun* 東門),[19] but their gestures mean only that they wish for their monarchs to become like the ancient Fuxi[20] and the Yellow Emperor,[21] to restore the peace in the world and to civilize the people. Therefore, even if in old age they retire to the woods, their mind-heart is still devoted to the country and the king; even when their body is decrepit, they never cease to think about advising the monarch. When their body travels far, their heart remains above the palace gate; hiding away from the world, they join the ranks of the loyal subjects. They have the mind-heart of exemplary scholars (*sagunja* 士君子). If the monarch is holy and sage and his people are of outstanding benevolence, when he is calling from afar by using noble words, if the summoned one does not return to society, this is against the manner of an exemplary scholar. How could one not change his mind and respond? However, it is not so for the great Buddhist master. From the "three realms of existence"[22] he makes his hoe, and from the "four modes of birth"[23] he makes his illusory world. He

---

18   Reference to the "Story of Bo Yi and Shu Qi". According to the *Book of Mencius*, The North Sea (*Beihe* 北海) is the place where Bo Yi and his brother retreated when fleeing from King Wu.

19   Reference to Mei Fu 梅福, a scholar of the Former Han dynasty (206 BCE – 8 CE) who retired from public duty after having been appointed as educational instructor and head of the Nanchang commandery and who submitted a few memorials criticizing the general Wang Feng during the reign of Emperor Cheng (r. 33 - 7 BCE). According to old stories, he hung his dignitary hat on the East Gate and left the service in protest.

20   Fuxi 伏羲, a mythological hero, who, together with his wife and sister Nüwa, is credited with the creation and civilization of the world and a few inventions, including the eight trigrams.

21   Huangdi 黃帝 or the Yellow Emperor is one of the Five Mythological Emperors of China (*Wudi* 五帝) and is considered a paragon of wisdom, whose reign, like that of the emperors Yao and Shun or the Duke of Zhou, was a golden age. He is a civilizing hero, who gifted the people with many inventions.

22   Reference to the Buddhist "three realms of *saṃsāra*" (*samyu* 三有 or *samgye* 三界), a triple dimensional world made of sensuous desire (*yok* 慾), form (*saek* 色), and formless or spirit (*musaek* 無色).

23   The Buddhist term *sasaeng* 四生 refers to the ways of coming into existence:(1) birth from the womb (*t'aesaeng* 胎生) for people and animals; (2) birth from an egg (*nansaeng* 卵生), as in the case of oviparous creatures—birds, fish and reptiles;

leaves this world serene and composed and quickly cuts off his ties to society, for he already forgot all feelings, he suppressed all thoughts about poverty or success in society. When he goes among people, his palanquin and parasol are not sumptuous, when he retires he cannot be faulted for turning his back to the country. His teachings awaken the people, making them cheer and cry. When the path can be taken to go, he does not hesitate to return, tranquil and peaceful, like the cry of a phoenix, like the emergence of a deer. He comes and goes the way the clouds and cranes are moving. What then does he have to do with this world and why would he take part in debating whether it is better to act or to retire?

[...]

Therefore, those who serve like the Buddhist master and inquire about the rites and the government and participate to the decisions of their time while pursuing their study and dissipating their doubts, their contribution is not limited [to just doing this], but they are the ones who transmit the immensurable treasure [of Buddhist teachings] to the world. When things are this way, the one in a high position will not be in danger, and the one in a low position will be obedient and not rebel. This way, the five constant virtues (*oryun* 五倫) will be respected to their utmost and the five statutory relations (*ojŏn* 五典) ensure the order to their utmost. Then, if the myriad things would be ruled as one, and the myriad people would have [proper] guidance, this would indeed be an unusual way of using this treasure.

---

(3) birth from moisture (*sŭpsaeng* 濕生), which refers to insects and worms; (4) metamorphic birth, or spontaneous birth (*hwasaeng* 化生), which is an attribute of celestial beings or hell-dwelling deities.

無思第一

　清寒子曰。古人之於爲道也。常惜寸陰。未嘗放逸。今之人。終朝
兀兀。無思無慮。何時徹悟。有客難之曰。夫道。自然無思無慮也。凡
有思慮者。妄也。可以道而思慮乎。曰無思無慮者。道之體也。精慮不
怠者。立功之要也。常觀世間之事。一不經慮。萬事瓦裂。況至眞無妄
之道。其可怠惰而得乎。故季文有三思之行。宜聖立九思之目。曾子記
慮得之語。夫子有遠慮之戒。自非天性聰明。無待勉強。孰能不思。且
人之氣質。有昏明愚智之不同。苟非孜孜兀兀。安得齊於上聖乎。必硏
精思慮。日鍊月磨。以造乎自得之域。然後可以言道者無思也無慮也。
客曰。方內之敎。禮術風規。粲然有序。三綱五常。八條九經。自始至
終。條理章然。自父子以至君臣。自格物以至平天下。自尊賢以至懷諸
侯。上自帝王。下及庶民。爲學有序。今日了一事。明日了一事。日漸
月磨。必至於聖而後已。故易贊精義入神之妙。傳記愼思明辨之功。使
天下之事。章章然有條不紊。然後可以居於世上。而不與鳥獸夷狄同
群。方外之士。坐斷世網。百慮俱閑。上無折腰於侯王。下絶致敬於親
戚。與鳥獸而同歡。以淡泊爲眞歸。何所留心乎。何所思慮乎。清寒子
曰。方外人之淡泊。固爾。已未得到向上田地。其可不思乎。夫世人稱
禪。是禪定安閑之意。未知禪字乃思修靜慮之稱。夫天地之間。人爲最
靈。智超萬物。雖顯晦殊塗。其可一日不學乎。其可一日不思乎。蓋學
而不思則罔。思而不學則殆。思非邪思。乃思其所以爲道。慮非狂慮。
乃慮其所以爲學。雖復彷徉戶庭。夷猶原野。目覩心思。以漸頤養。
未嘗敢廢於學也。故登山則思學其高。臨水則思學其清。坐石則思學其
堅。看松則思學其貞。對月則思學其明。萬像齊現於瑩然方寸之間。而
各有所長。我皆悉而學之。精硏其妙。以入於神。吾不知爲道之窮域
也。

　山林第二
　清寒子曰。古人雖處山林。飮峯啄澗。必整規矩。故出而爲一代師。
動而爲萬世法。今則淨室明朗。簟席溫慇。弛慢怠惰。何能進修。客又
難之曰。規矩準繩。處世之常典。放曠散誕。山林之逸態。焉有掬溪
而飮。煮藜而食。身在樗散之地。而顧視規繩乎。清寒子笑而問之曰。
爾所謂規繩者何。曰。法度也。曰。法度者何。曰。慇其衣冠。尊其瞻
視。如執玉。如奉盈。有威可畏。謂之威。有儀可則。謂之儀。彼山
林之士。麻衣襤縷。僅容於踵膝。葛巾岸倒。不庇於鬢耳。焉有束帶
矜莊。衣冠儼然之理乎。且　鹿魚鳥。不是立軌之群。巖壑危深。非可

憨步之場。所言規矩。何所施哉。清寒子大噱曰。子徒知在世之方準。
不悟出世之繩律也。姑爲汝敎之。夫道無方軌。法無定準。子知飾身
之有度。不知大道之標格者也。蓋士之所守者道也。所操者志也。守其
道則雖無服飾。而威儀有章。操其志則事越規矩。而法度粲然。斷髮文
身。雖非象服之宜。孔子稱其德。鼓刀飯牛。豈有將相之容。齊桓舉爲
輔。此其規矩也。方外之士。守道不篤。立志不確。則飢困適足以棄
吾命。窮迫亦足以壞此生耳。焉有掬溪而飲。優三詔之寵。採蘩而食。
足一生之歡哉。必也飯穊茹蔬。而其量則廓如也。蓽楣衡門。而其志則
泊如也。陶鑄唐虞。俛仰古今。逍遙自然之勢。恬淡無爲之場。身不待
規矩。而人望之儼然。資不擇草木。而物仰之彌高。魚鳥猿獲。感其
德。人天衆庶。慕其道。夫如是。故可以爲一代師萬世則。客曰。有道
之士。跧伏山林。大忘人世。未嘗以一利動其心。以一榮虧其節。奈何
遽以一代師萬世則。議彼方外乎。清寒子曰。爾之言。美則美矣。未知
有道者之爲有道也。蓋有道之士。跧伏山林。非所願也。行道於世。亦
非志願也。可以行則行。可以止則止。有煨芋垂涕而長往者。亦有欣然
曳杖而出山者。時而後動。動不乖其道。信然後言。言不戾其化。不爲
利。故其言硬而直。不愛名。故其事正而嚴。不偷生。故其談足以動皇
王。不畏死。故其法可以警塵機。王侯禮敬。而不爲高。瓦合輿儓。而
不爲卑。異端百毀。而其道愈堅。邪謗交攻。而其宗不磨。夫是之謂有
道之士。而一代師。萬世則。則其道德之滂沱。有不能掩者耳。非如自
衒自媒。以邀榮利者之比也。

三請第三

客曰。古者有高僧。有三請不赴者。有影不出山者。無乃違於化物。
而獨善其身乎。且世之賢士。隱於畎畝版築之間。有三聘而出者。有一
招而赴者。爲行道也。爲蒼生也。爲致君於堯舜之上也。在俗士尙爾。
況誠如上所謂高僧乎。若有識者聞。則不免懷寶迷邦之譏。則如之何。
清寒子曰。是何言之固滯也。覺皇之法。在於淸淨寡欲。不與物爭。故
卷於山阿則其道尊。行於人世則其法嚴。世溷而不遵其法。非可憂。時
平而盡行其道。非可歡。以道而處也。雖窮居山野。不改其樂。以法而
出也。雖對御談經。不驕其志。優哉游哉。無縛無拘。此高僧之去就
也。在賢士則不然。幼而學之。壯而欲行。不幸世亂時危。國君無從諫
之心。朝廷交豺虺之跡。或投竿北海之濱。或掛冠東門之上。而其志願
則欲致君於羲軒。濟世於雍熙而已。故雖投老山林。而長懷君國之心。
委身俳優。而不忘匡輔之懷。身雖去矣。而心懸魏闕之上。迹已遁矣。
而志在藎臣之列。此士君子之立心也。若主聖臣賢。旁求俊彥。而猶
大語高談。終不出世。乖士君子之願。安得不幡然而起哉。在高僧則不

然。以三有爲一家。以四生爲一幻。淡然離世。翛然絕俗。旣忘彼此之
情。又絕窮達之懷。出無軒蓋之華。隱無負國之乖。談話可以牖人。則
激而揚之。世道可以去矣。則浩然而返。坦坦然怡怡然。如鳳之鳴。
如麟之現。自去自來。如雲如鶴。夫何關係之有。而參於現晦之論哉。
曰。然則其道恬淡。乏輔君濟民之術。安能爲一代師。萬世則哉。且所
師者何物。所則者何事。曰。所師者。心也。夫心者。虛明洞照。出入
無時。莫知其鄉。迷之則狂蕩而忘返。悟之則圓明而匪失。自非上智之
質大過人者。困知力行。猶且不逮。而所謂伊人者。則洞徹深源。研窮
萬化。操守未形之前。神用無窮之變。定慧均等。精探萬法之根。智行
兩全。默契冥濛之始。語其神也。則毫髮充於大千。語其妙也。則性相
融於三際。語其道也。則鬼神所莫窺。語其德也。則龍天所欽仰。然則
其師事也。非徒問禮問政。決當時之務。受業解惑。資一時之用而已。
實乃得受用無盡之寶。傳萬世無疆之珍耳。以此在上。則高而不危。以
此在下。則順而不悖。施之五倫。則五倫其敍。制之五典。則五典極其
秩。乃至統理萬事。帥御萬夫。何莫非此寶之妙用乎。

References

Primary sources

Kim Sisŭp. *Collected Writings of Maewŏldang* (*Maewŏldang chip* 梅月堂集), Hōsa Bunko, *Maewŏltangchip* in Korean Classics Database, 1583: https://db.itkc. or.kr/dir/item?itemId=MO#/dir/node?dataId=ITKC_MO_0069A_ 0190_010_0030.

_____. *Kugyŏk Maewŏltang chŏnjip*, Pŏnyŏk p'yŏnjip Kangwŏn Hyangt'o Munhwa Yŏn'guhoe Kangwŏn-do, 2000.

Secondary sources

Ames, Roger T., Rosemont Jr., Henry, trans. *The Analects of Confucius: A Philosophical Translation*. New York: The Random House Publishing Group, 1998.

Ch'oe, Kwi-muk. *Kim Sisŭp-ŭi sasang-gwa kŭl ssŭgi*. Seoul: Somyŏng Ch'ulp'an, 2001.

Digital Dictionary of Buddhism, http://www.buddhism-dict.net/.

Lao Zi, *Daodejing*. https://ctext.org/dao-de-jing/zh.

Muller, Charles A. trans. *The Doctrine of the Mean*. http://www.acmuller.net/condao/docofmean.html.

ROMAN PAŞCA (KYOTO UNIVERSITY)

A PORTRAIT OF THE PHILOSOPHER AS A MATURE MAN
Andō Shōeki on Nature, Language and Himself

Translator's notes

Andō Shōeki (安藤昌益), one of the most enigmatic figures in the history of Japanese philosophy, lived and was active in the first half of the eighteenth century (1703–1762). Not much is known about his life until the 1740s, when he (re)surfaces in Hachinohe, a fief in northern Japan, where the records show he had a practice as a town physician. Hachinohe is considered by some the birthplace of his philosophy, as this is where he starts expounding his ideas and musings about the world in general, and about nature in particular.[1] Over the years, he gathered around him a small following of a handful of disciples—who listened to his talks and helped him transcribe his works—but he was never a major figure in the intellectual landscape of the time. He remained the "odd one out," as he was never part of any of the dominant traditions or schools of the Tokugawa period, a somewhat isolated, lonely figure, yet a profoundly original thinker.

Most scholars and commentators consider Shōeki to be a philosopher of nature, or a naturalist philosopher, and this categorization is correct for the most part: his major work, *Shizen shin'eidō* 自然真営道 ("The Way of Functioning of the Truth of Nature"), is undoubtedly one of the richest, most complex and most systematic texts dealing with nature as a philosophical concept written in the Edo period.[2] Yet I would argue that Shōeki is much more than that: he is also a social

---

1 Toshinobu Yasunaga, *Andō Shōeki: Social and Ecological Philosopher of Eighteenth-Century Japan* (New York: Weatherhill, 1992), 32.

2 The interpretations of Shōeki's philosophy range from "naturalist philosopher" (Berthrong 2003) to "pioneer ecologist" (Tsuzuki 2000), moving across an entire spectrum of diverse and sometimes contradictory readings which include, for instance, the idea that he put forth a "utopian ideal" (De Bary 2005), or the argu-

philosopher, a vehement critic of the *status quo* of the time, ceaselessly castigating the shogunate and extoling the farmers; he is also a philosopher of language, pondering on the purpose and meaning of language, letters, the act of writing, and books; he is also a humanist philosopher, preoccupied with the value of human beings, their freedom, their agency, their identity or their sense of self, etc. His writings cover a wide array of topics, from detailed and sometimes contradictory descriptions of the intricate mechanisms of nature, to fables and parables where he lets other creatures speak their mind about the human realm, to bulky lexicons and dictionaries where almost all etymologies and explanations are quite phantasmagorical, to anatomical and botanical drawings, some without the slightest shred of scientific grounding, meant to supplement and support his philosophical discourse.

This seemingly incongruent mix of themes and motifs is further complicated by Shōeki's reluctance to divide or categorize his preoccupations and concerns in any way, which creates a somewhat chaotic amalgam in which even the shortest sections can contain references to several important philosophical topics. The text, therefore, is definitely not easy to read, not easy to digest, and not easy to translate. Navigating through the multitude of concepts and notions that Shōeki juggles with; identifying all the possible allusions and innuendoes in the text; clarifying the meaning of all the words for which he proposes original, alternative spellings or readings; discerning the (intended) meaning of all the ideographs and readings he invents himself—these are all difficult tasks that represent a challenge for any reader, translator, or philosopher. But the task, arduous and sinuous as it may be, is also extremely rewarding, as what emerges at the end of the process, after peeling off all the layers, is an undiluted concentrate of philosophy in its purest form, transcending categorizations and borders, relevant not only for the intellectual landscape of Edo period Japan but for world philosophies in general. And, I venture to argue, an excellent example of what Hadot calls "philosophy as a way of life."[3]

---

ment that he advocated a "return to a completely agrarian economy" (Tipton 2008). For a detailed analysis of these interpretations, cf. Pașca 2017.

3   Pierre Hadot, *Philosophy as a Way of Life* (Oxford: Blackwell Publishing, 1995), 265.

Following is a translation of sections 7 through 16 from Shōeki's text *Taijokan* 大序巻 ("The Great Introduction"). The fragments are included in *Andō Shōeki Zenshū* ("The Complete Works of Andō Shōeki," henceforth abbreviated as ASZ), volume I, pages 96–112. The *Taijokan* consists of a total of 25 sections of varied lengths and, in spite of its title, it is actually the last of Shōeki's writings—in fact, as Terao Gorō shows,[4] it is highly likely that he died while compiling this text, which would explain the differences in composition and type of discourse: while sections 1 through 15 are written in the first person (with Shōeki referring to himself by using the pronoun *yo* 予), sections 16 through 25 start with the words *Senkaku ga iwaku* 仙确ガ日ク ("This is what Senkaku says"),[5] indicating that Senkaku wrote them—or, at least, annotated and collated Shōeki's drafts. *Taijokan* contains *in nuce* all the major themes of Shōeki's thought, from his view of nature to his rather radical understanding of language—it is, as Terao puts it, a "crystallization" of his philosophy. However, since it was meant to be an introduction to *Shizen shin'eidō*, it should be taken as a supplement to it—in fact, most of the sections from *Taijokan* remain rather cryptic and inscrutable when read independently, without the detailed explanations, examples and parables from *Shizen shin'eidō*.

The fragments selected here should, I believe, be read as examples of the "crystallization" mentioned above, as they all contain, in a nutshell, several overarching themes in Shōeki's philosophy. The first theme is, of course, the world of nature—or, as Shōeki puts it, the world of Living Truth—with its whole intricate, dynamic system or relationships among its different components: "spontaneity, the four directions, advancement and retreat, mutual natures, the eight energies, the circulation of the three flows, and the subtle actions" and so on and so forth. The second theme—second but not secondary by any means—is that of writing, with a particular focus on letters and books and their (true) meaning and intent. In sections 7, 8, 10, and 12 in particular, Shōeki

---

4   Terao Gorō 寺尾五郎, *Andō Shōeki no tatakai* (安藤昌益の戦い, Andō Shōeki's Fights) (Tōkyō: Nōsan gyoson bunka kyōkai, 1978), passim.

5   Kamiyama Senkaku 神山仙确 (? –1783) was a physician in the Hachinohe fief in northern Japan, where Shōeki also practiced medicine. He was also one of the few disciples Shōeki had, and some commentators attribute the compilation and editing of *Shizen shin'eidō* to him.

defends and explains his seemingly paradoxical position of using letters to expose his ideas while, at the same time, constantly and vehe-
mently vituperating them, thus showing us yet another facet of himself
as a philosopher preoccupied with metalanguage and metaphilosophy
as well. A third theme identifiable here is what I would call the "legacy
for the future": we see a philosopher (and his disciple, for that matter)
concerned with the destiny of his ideas and pondering on their impact
on future generations. As such, he also hints at what the purpose of the
whole endeavor of philosophy is—simply put, to bring peace through
a thorough understanding of the ways of the world. A fourth theme—
last but not least, and somehow tying all the knots and loose ends of all
the others—would be that of the embeddedness of the Way of Nature,
i.e., the understanding that this "Way" of the "Living Truth" is not
something out of reach, not something *external* to us that we should
strive to reach and attain; instead, it is to be found *within* us, internal,
embedded within us since birth, and in order to realize it we should
first and foremost look within, and reflect on ourselves. This is a recur-
ring theme in Shōeki's work. In *Tōdōshinden* 統道真伝 ("The true unified transmission of the Way"), for example, he talks about the human
being as a microcosm, i.e. a miniature-scale embodiment of the whole
universe—and it may serve as a reminder for all of us that examining
the world (of nature) should in fact begin with an examination of our
own selves, our own humanity.

As for Shōeki's discourse, it must be said *ab initio* that his style of
writing is never linear or straightforward. Sentences are sometimes
long and convoluted, and sometimes short and almost cryptic; there
are numerous repetitions and divagations that render many passages
confusing and inconsistent; there are countless references to a whole
range of texts from a wide array of intellectual traditions—from
Chinese classics to ancient Japanese chronicles or Buddhist scriptures—and deciphering them is problematic as Shōeki (intentionally
or accidentally) frequently misquotes or misunderstands them; the
established writing system is constantly challenged and pushed to
its limits as Shōeki keeps coming up with new, freshly coined ideographs or readings with almost every page turn, etc. That being said,
his writing is by no means an incomprehensible word salad; despite
its shortcomings, or perhaps incongruities is a better term, it is def-

initely one of the most systematic and thorough discourses in pre-modern Japanese philosophy, revealing a philosopher determined to put forth a coherent, all-encompassing, original system of thought, while remaining acutely aware of, and preoccupied with, the place that system might inhabit within the broader framework of the East Asian intellectual traditions.

One last thing to note about the way in which Shōeki constructs his discourse is his use of dialogue as a pretext to expound his ideas; needless to say, this rhetorical device is not specific to Shōeki. We find it in Daoist parables, in Buddhist commentaries, in Confucian texts, and even in ancient Greek philosophy. As can be seen in sections 7, 11, and 13, Shōeki conjures up an indefinite "somebody" (*aru hito* 或人) and then proceeds to engage in a conversation with them, in which he reveals the truth about the Way—and inevitably, that "somebody" who challenged or misunderstood the truth ends up by leaving, crushed under the weight of the argument and covered in shame. This *aru hito* is, of course, a metaphorical representation of the uninitiated, of the lay person who has not yet grasped the Living Truth and still needs to do some introspection in order to attain it.

The last section translated here is the first one in the structure of the *Taijokan* attributed to Senkaku and, as such, its scope and theme are slightly different. We do find the same major topics of Shōeki's philosophy in this excerpt as well, yet the perspective is de-centered: since the author of this section is Senkaku, his point of view is that of the disciple writing about his master and describing him in a way Shōeki himself would perhaps never have done. My choice of including this section was motivated first and foremost by the fact that, through the gaze of the disciple, it opens a window into Shōeki as a human being, into his life, his habits, his way of acting, and into his dialectical methods and his philosophical practice. And beyond the enthusiastic adulatory overtones, Senkaku paints the portrait of a man who, simply put, practices what he preaches, someone for whom understanding the Way of the Living Truth is not just about transmitting it on to the next generations, but about *living* it. Senkaku's depiction of Shōeki reiterates and reinforces the topics and *topoi* that transpire from the dialogues with *aru hito*, while at the same time revealing a thinker for whom philosophy was indeed a way of life.

Taijokan (大序巻)

"The Great Introduction"

Section 7

Somebody (或人) asked me this question: "You say that letters and writings are mere tools used to steal the Way of Heaven (転道),[6] and the biggest enemy of the Truth of Heaven (転真)[7]; but in fact you yourself make use of letters in your writings. Why do you use letters if they are means of exploitation?" This is what I answered: "When you build a house, you will inevitably use a wedge. Let's suppose you have a faulty house. If you want to rebuild it, you have to take out the wedge and demolish it. Yet if you cannot remove the wedge, you need to put in a new one, then remove the old wedge, and then build a new house to replace the defective one. The books I am writing now are much like that new wedge. In order to correct the errors[8] of the schol-

---

6   Not satisfied with the ideograph traditionally used in both Chinese and Japanese texts to render the concept of Heaven (*ten* 天), Shōeki constantly uses, throughout his texts, the alternative spelling 転, which has the same reading but a different (original) meaning: "to revolve," "to roll," "to fall," sometimes even "to change." With this spelling, he aims to convey a sense of dynamism: in his view, the old, regular *ten* is too static, suspended high above Earth and disconnected from it, existing as a separate realm; whereas his *ten* is constantly moving, in a neverending back-and-forth with Earth, separate yet inseparable like the two sides of the same coin. *Tendō*, the Way of Heaven, refers here broadly to all the laws that regulate nature in its entirety.

7   The Truth of Heaven (*tenshin* 転真) and the Living Truth (*kasshin*, or *ikite makoto* 活真) are both alternative terms for nature (*shizen* 自然), which Shōeki uses interchangeably. They are not perfect synonyms, though, as *tenshin* designates nature in its entirety, as a unitary whole, while *kasshin* refers rather to its instantiations or materializations in smaller-scale, sometimes concrete, contexts.

8   For what I translated as "error" and "erroneous," Shōeki uses the word *ayamari*, which he spells as 失り, with the ideograph for "losing." His intention seems to be to suggest that these *ayamari* are not mere mistakes, but represent in fact something

ars of the past and to remove the erroneous letters (which correspond to the old wedge), I use letters as a new wedge. My sole purpose is to destroy the old books, which are the very root of exploitation and conflict, and to create a world of the Living Truth (活真), peaceful, without exploitation and without conflict, that would last well into the future, for ever, for eternity (後後・永永・無限二). That is why I am using an error to remove another error, thus bringing to light the True Way (真道).[9] If you want to interrogate a thief, the best thing is to have another thief do it. Much in the same way, in order to destroy the erroneous letters and books which are the root of exploitation, I have to use erroneous letters and books. This allows me to demolish them completely. So, I am only using letters as a device, provisionally. He who starts a war, you defeat him by war. Of course, it is an error to start a war. And of course, it is also an error to wage war in order to defeat somebody who started a war. Yet sometimes you can only remove an error with another error. That's why I make use of erroneous letters and books in order to thoroughly destroy erroneous letters and books. I use erroneous letters as a device to remove all the errors from the past. There is nothing erroneous in that, is there?" The person who asked the question closed their mouth and left.

Section 8

The fact that I use letters to write about the True Way of Functioning (真営道)[10] does not mean that I endorse letters. My purpose is to expose the nonsense of the old writings, and to bring to light the True Way of Functioning. All books and letters are self-serving contrap-

---

more serious, i.e., a deviation from the True Way of nature, whereby something of importance is lost.

9   For Shōeki the True Way can only be the Way of Nature, of course. Yet this is not a "way" in the Daoist, or Confucian sense of the term, of a principle that is the source of all existence, as it rather refers to a profound understanding of the intricate and delicate relationships established between the various elements of nature, and of the fact that living in accordance with them is the only possible option.

10 *Shin'eidō* also appears in the title of Shōeki's major work and is a central subject for his philosophy. This "True Way of Functioning" refers to the inner workings of nature.

tions meant to steal the subtle way of the Living Truth, and as such they are the greatest evil of this world (転下ノ大怨). But ordinary people (世人), maybe because they were accustomed to using them for a long time, venerate them as if they were deities. That is utter stupidity and delusion (愚惑).[11] I am the one who, for the first time, made known the fact that letters and books are just tools meant to steal the Way of Heaven and a big nuisance to the world. That's why the ordinary people who read my books are surprised and incredulous. Yet you should not doubt, and you should not be confused. For as long as letters and books exist, there will be many—people who don't cultivate anything and rob the fruit of the others' labor[12]—in the world who will use them to spread [certain] teachings and to put themselves in a higher position, and thus the roots of conflict in this world will never be eliminated. Therefore, the erasing and discarding of each and every letter is in fact an act of great service (奉公) toward the Living Truth. That is the reason why I'm exposing all the errors in the letters and books of old by using erroneous letters. Medical treatises, for example, don't understand either the mutual natures (互性)[13] at work in the causes of the diseases, or the mutual natures of the effects of the herbal medicines. All of them are completely erroneous. I expose them by using erroneous letters so as to get rid of letters and books, and to demonstrate the embeddedness of the mutual natures of the causes of the diseases, and of the effects of the medicines. Confucian

---

11   Shōeki uses this term (read *guwaku*) elsewhere as well, always in contexts where he criticizes the other philosophical traditions and their legacy.

12   The term used in the original is *fukōtōshoku* (不耕盗食), which is in fact a variant of the much more common *fukōdonshoku* (不耕貪食), "non-cultivation and insatiable greed." The only difference between the two is the third ideograph, *tō* ("stealing") vs. *don* ("devouring"). *Fukō* is a key term in Shōeki's system of thought, representing the opposite of *chokkō* ("straight cultivation"), which covers a wide variety of actions and behaviors, from tilling the land to living in accordance with the principles of nature. *Fukō* is "non-cultivation," i.e. a deliberate transgression of the Way.

13   "Mutual natures" (*gosei*) is a term coined by Shōeki to designate the reciprocal embeddedness of all things existing in nature, from concrete things such as human beings to abstract entities such as the flows of energy. It is predicated on the idea that the essence of any entity is embedded, or contained, within another (which would normally be its opposite), and that, hence, they cannot exist independently from each other. A recurrent example in these sections is the relationship between light and darkness.

and Buddhist texts, the writings of Laozi and Zhuangzi, Shinto[14] books—none of them is an exception. Once you have removed the old wedge with the new one, you have no use for wedges anymore. Once you have completely erased all the errors of the old texts with erroneous letters, you have no use for letters anymore. A person who does not let go of the wedge even after it has been removed cannot know what the wedge used to be before it became a tool for building a house. A person who destroys erroneous books with erroneous letters and then still remains attached to them cannot escape confusion for the rest of his life. Therefore, the fact that I am writing this book using erroneous letters is only because I want to destroy letters and books, and to indicate the True Way of Functioning. And I am not doing this for myself, but for future generations.

Section 9

I am only writing this book now because I want to reveal everything about nature, the Living Truth, spontaneity, the four directions, advancement and retreat, mutual natures, the eight energies, the circulation of the three flows, and the subtle actions,[15] without adding even an ounce of my own knowledge based on discrimination (分別知). I only talk about things that the sages of old, Buddha, Laozi, Zhuangzi, all the doctors, all the Shintoists, all the Buddhists, all the wisemen and all the scholars[16] never talk about because they have not understood them yet. All the old theories have already been discussed

---

14 The term in the original is *kannagi* (巫), which designates the shaman-like priests and priestesses in the Shintō tradition.

15 This part, at first sight an almost random list of esoteric and vague concepts, can be read as the most concentrated abstract of Shōeki's understanding of nature. It contains almost all the key concepts of his vision, and the order of the elements in the list also points to the relations between them. A slightly more detailed explanation is also included in Section 16.

16 The term "sages" (*sei* 聖, or *seijin* 聖人) refers, first and foremost, to Confucius, but it can also mean all Confucian commentators and, by extension, all ruling elites whose justification of authority is inspired by Confucianism. The "wisemen" (*ken* 賢) and "scholars" (*gakusha* 学者) are all the authors and thinkers who comment on and interpret the the texts of the various doctrines. Shōeki uses these terms in a derogatory sense.

to exhaustion in the old books. To write again about them would do nothing but add [more] to the confusion. So I will not write a single letter about the old theories. I will just talk about the eight energies, mutual natures, and the circulation of the three flows.

Section 10

A sage once said: "Cultivate your body, keep your house in order, govern the country and make the world a peaceful place."[17] Many scholars revere this saying. But is there anything to revere about it? In a year with a bad harvest, all these scholars of non-cultivation and insatiable greed have no way of cultivating their body, so they suffer from hunger and they prey on those who practice straight cultivation (直耕ノ衆人)[18] or otherwise they would starve to death. Seeing them, those who practice straight cultivation say this: "Scholars say they should be revered. And you would think that, even in a bad year when there is not enough produce, they would not starve or freeze, but in fact they suffer from hunger even before us. When you see them like that, you realize that scholars, letters, and books are completely useless for human life. Quite the contrary, they do nothing but damage to human life. Letters and books are truly abominable!" And so, all the adepts of Confucianism, Buddhism, medicine, Laozi, Zhuangzi, Shinto and other self-serving laws—those who do not cultivate anything, rob the fruit of the others' labor, and occupy themselves only with letters and books—earn the contempt of ordinary people, who have no [knowledge of] letters or books (無字・無書); and they are incapable of uttering a single word in response. And that is because all the disciplines relying on letters and books are, from the very beginning, nothing more than offensive contraptions designed

---

17   The quote in the original is in fact a paraphrase of a short fragment from Confucius' text *The Great Learning* (大學). The next sentence is probably an allusion to Zhu Xi (朱子), the philosopher who advocated the inclusion of *The Great Learning* in the Four Books, the essence of the Confucian canon.

18   In this context, Shōeki most likely refers to farmers, whom he considered to be closest to nature because they practiced "straight cultivation" in its sense of physical labor—tilling the land, planting the seeds, harvesting the crop, etc. For Shōeki, these were essential actions for ensuring the sustenance of human beings.

to steal the Way of Heaven. When you can't even cultivate your own body, how can you govern and pacify a country or the whole world? Those who do not understand this are precisely the Confucian and Buddhist scholars. That is why letters and books are the greatest evil of this world.

Section 11

Somebody asked me this question: "In today's world, wherever you may go, you only find deceptive words and deceptive actions (偽談・偽行). Why are there no true words and true actions?" This is what I answered: "The sages of old appeared and established their five laws,[19] teaching deceptive words and thus stealing the Way of Heaven and the entire world. Buddha appeared and taught deceptive words, and about the expedient means (方便), placing himself on a high pedestal and devouring insatiably all the alms he received. Laozi appeared and taught the deceptive words 'if you cultivate your spirit, you will not die,' and he also devoured everything. Zhuangzi appeared and he told parables and misleading things, and he also devoured everything. Those who wrote medical treatises appeared,[20] fabricating and spreading falsehoods without a shred of evidence, killing people for a living, and they also devoured everything. Shōtoku Taishi appeared, established the three laws[21] and fabricated deceptive words. They all

---

19   Shōeki only uses the term "law" (*hō* 法) in a negative, disparaging sense, sometimes even giving it the reading *koshiraegoto*, which actually means "fabrication." For him, laws can only be self-serving and egotistic, an infringement upon the principles of nature. The "five laws" mentioned here might be a reference to the five Confucian virtues (benevolence 仁, righteousness 義, propriety 理, wisdom 智, and trustworthiness 信), which Shōeki criticizes as mere falsities whose only purpose is to institute hierarchies and justify authority.

20   This a reference to the authors of the "Inner Canon of the Yellow Emperor" (*Kōtei daikei* 黄帝内経 in Japanese), a collection of treatises that represented the quintessential doctrinal source for Chinese medicine (Unschuld 2003). Shōeki discusses the canon in detail in *Tōdōshinden* 統道真伝 ("The true unified transmission of the Way"), his second major text.

21   Shōeki considered Shōtoku Taishi to be the founder of Shintoism—in *Tōdōshinden*, he denounces what he sees as an unjustified emphasis on the number three in Shintoism ("three major gods," "three sacred treasures," etc.), so this sentence might be a reference to that. At the same time, it might also be a pun, a play on the reading

pretended to be teaching by using deceptive words. This is the cause for the spread of deceptive words and deceptive actions throughout the world. And letters, books, and all the disciplines based on them are responsible for this. That is why they are the evil of this world."

Section 12

Somebody asked me this question: "The value of a book is determined based on its phrasing. And phrasing in the old books is indeed outstanding. Whereas the sentences you are writing right now are deplorable. Why don't you try to make them better?" This is what I answered: "You talk about phrasing, but you don't understand the Way. You have no qualification to consider my writing deplorable. After all, sentences are nothing more than vessels used to discuss the Way. Even if the vessel is execrable, once you have tasted its content and understood the Way, there is no use for it anymore. That vessel is something that is only used temporarily. It is exactly the same with sentences. Once you utter them and understand their meaning, they become useless. They, too, are only used temporarily. You claim that the phrasing of the people of old is outstanding, but do you yourself know the reason why?" The person responded: "No, I don't." [I continued:] "Well, then do you know the reason why my sentences are deplorable?" "No, I don't." "That means you don't know what makes a sentence outstanding or deplorable. So how can you criticize me? All the letters are mere vessels meant to steal the Way of Heaven. He who doesn't know that and likes letters, is a completely deluded fool who also likes stealing the Way. That's why among those who like the poems and the prose of the ancient times there is not one who understands the principle of mutual natures. Sentences are not meant to be polished and refined. Their purpose is just to apprehend a meaning. That's the reason why in this book of mine, *The True Way of Functioning*, I don't embellish my sentences—I only want to describe the

---

of the words "three laws" (三法) and "three treasures" (三宝), both of them *sanpō* in Japanese. The "three treasures" is a syntagm that appears in the Seventeen-article Constitution (604), attributed to Shōtoku Taishi, where it refers to the Buddha, the (Buddhist) law, and the clergy.

Way of Functioning [of nature]. Hence, I don't polish my sentences. I want all those who read my book to ignore the phrasing and instead to understand the subtle way of the mutual natures and the functioning of the [Living] Truth. If you too want to know the True Way, then you should ignore the sentences, as they are just vessels for stealing. Or do you prefer to revere sentences and endorse stealing?" The person who asked the question felt a cold sweat, blushed with shame, and left immediately.

Section 13

Somebody asked me this question: "When you claim that Heaven-and-Earth are one, that man and woman form the human being together, that there should be no differentiation[22] between superior and inferior, good and bad, nobles and commoners, is that not just self-vaunting designed to mock the sages and Buddha? How can you do such a thing?" This is what I answered: "You talk about mocking the sages, but isn't Laozi already doing that? When he writes 'when the Great Way is abandoned, benevolence and righteousness arise,'[23] these are harsh words that mock all the sages of old. Even Zhuangzi, in the 'Outer Chapters'[24] of his own writings, considers the sages to be big thieves. That's terribly disparaging. Yet even if Laozi and Zhuangzi both deride the sages, they still remain [men] of non-cultivation and insatiable greed, thus committing the same offense of stealing the Way of Heaven, exactly like the sages. Deriding the sages without being aware of this is nothing but self-complacent drivel. When I say that there should be no differentiation between superior and inferior,

---

22 The term in the original is *nibetsu naki* (二別無キ), which means "no differentiation/distinction (into two)." Shōeki often uses it to emphasize the fact that nature is one single totality, undivided and indivisible, and that nothing can exist outside of it.

23 The line is from Chapter 18 of the *Tao Te Ching* 道徳経 (*Dōtokukyō* in Japanese), one of the fundamental Daoist texts, ascribed to Laozi. The implication here is that benevolence 仁 and righteousness 義, which are Confucian virtues, are not part of the Way.

24 Traditionally, the *Zhuangzi* is divided into three parts: the "Inner Chapters" (内篇), the "Outer Chapters" (外篇), and the "Mixed Chapters" (雑篇).

based on the subtle ways of the mutual natures and of *shizen*—such as Heaven-and-Earth as one, or man and woman fused together to form the human being—my purpose is not to deride the sages. I merely want to bring to light the subtle ways of nature, the Living Truth, and mutual natures. The fact that the sages devised private laws based on the distinction between superior and inferior happened because their knowledge was biased, and because they could not understand the True Way of mutual natures. Why would I even bother to deride them?" The person who asked the question left immediately, foaming at the mouth.

Section 14

When Fuxi[25] had just become emperor and come to stand above all, he had somebody catch a mantis and—perhaps because he was too blasé about all his glory—put it in a cage, planning to use it as a pastime. One day, he had the mantis taken out of the cage, set it down beside him and said: "This insect is so pitiful! Feed it some rice and soup!" The mantis smiled complacently and replied: "Oh you, emperor, you probably want to feed me just to show me some benevolence (仁). And yet the food you want to give me is no doubt from the grains and seeds produced by the farmers through straight cultivation. If you did not steal the Way of Heaven with your non-cultivation and insatiable greed, you would not have a single grain of rice of your own. You would probably try to give me the surplus left from what you extorted from those who practice straight cultivation. I may be nothing more than an insect, but I am definitely not one to eat something that has been stolen. You should really strive to discern what the Way is. All human beings under Heaven are just one and the same.[26] Since you were also born into this world where people are supposed to be equal, you should practice straight cultivation and get your food and clothing by living in accordance with

---

25 Fuxi 伏義 is a mythological divine being, considered to be one of the ancestors of mankind, and the first emperor of China.

26 Given the context, by "... are just one" (*tada hitori nari* 只一人ナリ), Shōeki most likely means "equal."

the Truth of Heaven. In this world where people are supposed to be equal, whom are you trying to govern as an emperor, for whom can you be an emperor? Because you steal the Way of Heaven with your non-cultivation and insatiable greed, you are in fact the chieftain of all the thieves in this world. Yet incapable of understanding this, you call yourself an emperor, you built a castle, named it Imperial Palace (禁中) and now you live in it. But that, in fact, means you are punished,[27] you are trapped in a cage. Whether you catch me and put me in a cage, or whether you live in the Imperial Palace, it's the same thing: a cage is still a cage. So you—who created your own self-serving laws and live within their constraints—caught me as I was playing around freely on the Heaven-given fields where I was born, put me in a cage and treated me as a criminal even though I committed no crime; therefore, it is in fact you who committed the crime. And if you think you committed no crime, that is just prejudice and delusion, which makes you inferior even to an insect. Since you are dominated by the karma of lateral [energy] (横業)[28] even during your lifetime, what awaits you after your death is the inevitable karma of deformation (形化ノ業) whereby you will be reborn exactly like me." Having said this, the mantis just flew away. This is not merely an allegory meant to disparage emperors, like one of Zhuangzi's deprecating parables; this is a manifestation of the True Way [telling us] that one who strays away from the subtle ways of the Living Truth and of the mutual natures is no better than an insect, who never strays away.

Section 15

[Somebody asked me this question:] "Among all the scholars of Confucianism, military art, medicine, Buddhism, Daoism and Shin-

---

27 The original is *imashime no naka,* which Shōeki writes as 禁ノ中, thus playing with the reading and meaning of the ideographs for "Imperial Palace."

28 In Shōeki's cosmology, human beings are sustained by the flow of descending energy *gyakki* 逆気, while the lateral energy ōki 横気 begets birds, beasts, crawling creatures and fishes. In this context, Fuxi is dominated by lateral energy, which makes him no better than the mantis—in a sense, he has lost his status as a human being. With a slightly different phrasing, the idea is reprised in section 16: "human beings fell into a state similar to that of the four types [of creatures]."

toism, why isn't there anyone who understands the subtle ways of the Living Truth?" This is what I answered: "Because they only study the biased, misleading teachings and writings of the sages from ancient times, of the Buddha, of the doctors, of Laozi and Zhuangzi, and of the Shintoists, thus failing to perceive the subtle way of the mutual natures, present before their very eyes and embedded in their very bodies, which leads them into prejudice and confusion. That is why they are incapable of understanding the subtle ways of the truth, which all human beings possess from birth. If they truly want to know the subtle ways of the Living Truth, they should rely on the Way embedded in their bodies and before their eyes, and acquire full knowledge of mutual natures, [as manifested for example in the relationship] between light and darkness. When you fully understand this, you will realize that the Living Truth of nature, beginningless and endless, and all the subtle movements of Heaven-and-Earth, of the sun, the moon and the stars, of the grains (穀), of the human beings (男女 *hito*),[29] of the four types [of creatures], and of the plants and trees, are the same as the subtle movements of the Living Truth within your own body. You don't have to make efforts to look for them very far away."

Section 16

This is what Senkaku says: "Ryōshi[30] is my teacher. He himself did not have any teachers, and he does not have any disciples. If you ask him about human beings or the Way, he will answer; but if you ask him about private matters, he will not respond. When I ask him about the Way he always responds, and I respect his answer as coming from a teacher. Let me tell you what I know about his personality.[31] He only talks about and brings to light the things that the

---

29   As I discussed in detail elsewhere (Paşca 2016), Shōeki insists on writing *hito*, the word for human being, with the two ideographs for man and woman. He considers *hito* to be a manifestation of mutual natures, where man and woman are fused together into an inseparable whole, like the two sides of the same coin.

30   Ryōshi 良子 and Ryōchū 良中 were the appellations most frequently used by Shōeki's disciples to refer to him.

31   The term in the original is *hitotonari* 為人, usually translated as "behavior" or "conduct."

sages, Buddha, Laozi, Zhuangzi or Shōtoku Taishi were not able to comprehend, and he never mentions a single line from the ancient books. He knows and observes the Way which is embedded [in all things], and the mutual natures [as manifested for example in the relationship] between light and darkness; he has exquisite knowledge (神知) and acts very quickly—he truly is a man of the Living Truth. His disposition is neither overbearing nor humble, and his looks are neither good nor bad. But with his spirit and his feelings (神情),[32] he fully understands nature, the living truth, and the subtle ways of the mutual natures. By perceiving the subtle way of the mutual natures, present before his eyes and embedded in his body, he knows very well that the fact that the Living Truth—beginningless and endless—created Heaven-and-Earth; the sun, the moon and the stars; the grains with all their ears and pods; human beings; the birds, the beasts, the crawling creatures and the fishes; the grasses and the trees; that [the Living Truth] is moving in three directions—descending, lateral, and ascending (通横逆)—thus engendering the eight energies which are all in a relation of mutual natures—all this is in fact nothing more than straight cultivation (直耕). He always respects straight cultivation and never forgets it. He is deeply saddened by the fact that human beings fell into a state similar to that of the four types [of creatures] (四類二罪落) because of the sages of old, Buddha, Laozi and their followers who, due to their non-cultivation and insatiable greed, stole the Way of the Living Truth by fabricating self-serving laws to institute hierarchies, thus creating a world of evil filled with moans of confusion and bewilderment. He is distressed at the thought that the future generations will have to endure exploitation and conflict for a long time and, as a way of practicing self-cultivation, he wrote a book about nature, its living truth and its subtle way of functioning, in order to explain the True Way to future generations, thus hoping to create a world of perpetual peace, without any exploitation and without any conflict. The fact that he lives his life in straight culti-

---

32   The ideograph 神 is most commonly used to designate *kami*, the Shinto deities, but Shōeki—for whom the existence of *kami* as transcendental entities is nonsensical—derails it into signifying "spirit," or "mind." In doing so, he plays on the Chinese-style reading of the character (*shin*), which in Japanese is identical to the reading of the character 心, meaning the "heart-mind."

vation brings about the True Way for one generation. Transmitting the True Way of Functioning to future generations by writing a book on it brings about eternal, infinite True Way and straight cultivation. This is what motivated him to keep writing the book about the Living Truth for dozens of years.

In his daily life and practice, he is extremely frugal. Aside from rice and soup in the morning and in the evening, he eats nothing else; he does not drink alcohol and he does not fool around with other women. If you ask him a question that strays away from the Way, he will not respond. Yet if it is something that is beneficial for people or for the Way, he does not wait to be questioned but starts speaking; he does not waste even a single minute, and never falters in acting according to the True Way. He never praises or slanders others, and he is never either arrogant or too humble. He never envies those above him, nor despises those below him; he does not revere, he does not demean, he does not flatter, he does not exploit. His household is neither poor nor rich, he does not borrow or lend money; he follows the private law whenever he gives or receives money, but does not allow himself to be too concerned with it.[33] When ordinary people compliment him, he is distressed [thinking] that he has become foolish; when they ridicule him, he is overjoyed [thinking] that he is not mistaken (不失). He knows very well that ridiculing or praising somebody is something only the fools, the wise men and the sages of old (愚・賢・聖) would do, never the Correct Man.[34] He has an exquisite ability to only look at a person's face once and fully understand what their state of mind is and how they behave and act. He does not teach anything except for the Way; but since the Way is embedded in each human being, he does not teach or learn about it.[35] He does not indulge or hate himself or

---

33   Probably a reference to the fact that Shōeki was a physician and, as such, he would sometimes accept payment from his patients.

34   Just like "man of the Living Truth" (活真人), which appeared earlier in the same section, the "Correct Man" (*seijin* 正人) is a term coined by Shōeki to designate a person who understands the principles of nature and lives in accordance with them by practicing straight cultivation. It is only used sporadically, and when it occurs it is usually in the same context with *seijin* 聖人 (the "sages"), intentionally creating a contrast between the two.

35   The idea that the Way is contained within each human being and, as such, does not need to/cannot be taught is also to be found in Daoism. The implication here is

others; he does not become either too intimate, or too distant; he does not flaunt his [acts of] filial piety, yet he does not neglect his duties. As for things for recreation and pleasure, such as music, songs, and other amusements, while he does see or hear them, he never lets his spirit be enraptured [by such things]. And if you ask him [about such things], it is clear that he does have some knowledge about them. If I do not ask him anything, he will not try to force his teachings on me, but when it comes to the embedded Way, he never falters in following it, no matter what people might ask or suggest him to do. He follows the ways and customs of the world when it comes to any exchanges of gifts (施受), yet he does not let his spirit be too concerned with such things. When somebody wants something, he will give it to them without hesitation, and if they do not want it, he will not try to force it upon them. Because he realizes that life and death are just manifestations of the mutual natures that underpin the advancement and retreat of the Living Truth, he does not celebrate life, nor fear death.

All over the beginningless and endless Heaven-and-Earth, in all the lands, in the present or in the past, I have never heard of, let alone seen, any other man like him. It is not impossible that there might be, but I for one have not heard of such a man, and it is highly unlikely [that he exists]. This is the true character of my teacher."

References

Primary sources

ASZ   *Andō Shōeki Zenshū* (安藤昌益全集, "Complete works of Andō Shōeki"). Tokyo: Nōsan gyoson bunka kyōkai, 1997.

Secondary sources

Berthrong, John. "Confucian Views of Nature." In *Nature Across Cultures: Views of Nature and the Environment in Non-Western Cultures.* Edited by H. Selin & A.

---

that each person should discover the Way within them by themselves, without the guidance of teachers and books.

Kalland, 373 – 392. Dordrecht: Kluwer Academic Publishers, 2003.

De Bary, William Theodore. *Sources of Japanese Tradition: From Earliest Times to 1600*, vol. 1. Columbia: Columbia University Press, 2005.

Hadot, Pierre. *Philosophy as a Way of Life*. Oxford: Blackwell Publishing, 1995.

Paşca, Roman. "Beyond Ecology and Utopia: Reframing Andō Shōeki's Philosophy." In *A Festschrift for Florentina Vişan*. Edited by L. Bălan & M. Zlotea, 313 –327. Bucharest: University of Bucharest Press, 2017.

_____. "*Homo Naturalis*: Andō Shōeki's Understanding of the Human Being." *Critical Perspectives on Japanese Philosophy*. Edited by Takeshi Morisato, 78–99. Nagoya: Nanzan Institute for Religion and Culture & Chisokudō Publications, 2016.

Terao Gorō 寺尾五郎. *Andō Shōeki no tatakai* 安藤昌益の闘い (Andō Shōeki's fights). Tokyo: Nōsan gyoson bunka kyōkai, 1978.

Tipton, Elise K. *Modern Japan: A Social and Political History*. New York: Routlegde, 2008

Unschuld, Paul U. *Huang Di Nei Jing Su Wen: Nature, Knowledge, Imagery in an Ancient Chinese Medical Text*. Berkeley: University of California Press, 2003.

Totman, Conrad. *Early Modern Japan*. Berkeley: University of California Press, 2003.

Tsuzuki Chūshichi. *The Pursuit of Power in Modern Japan, 1825–1995*. Oxford: Oxford University Press, 2000.

Yasunaga, Toshinobu. *Andō Shōeki: Social and Ecological Philosopher of Eighteenth-Century Japan*. New York: Weatherhill, 1992.

Tanabe Hajime

ON CONFUCIANIST ONTOLOGY

Translated by Rossa Ó Mureartaig

Notes on Translation

Tanabe Hajime's (田辺元 1885-1962) essay *On Confucianist Ontology* (儒教的存在論に就いて) was originally written as part of a fest-schrift entitled *Collection of Essays on Chinese Studies to Commemorate Professor Takase's Sixtieth Birthday* (高瀬博士還暦記念志那学論叢) (Tokyo: Kōbundō, 1928) produced in honor of Takase Takejirō (高瀬武次郎1869–1950), a renowned scholar of Chinese philosophy who wrote under the penname of Takase Seiken (高瀬惺軒).[1] The introduction states, "December 16th, 1928, is in fact the 60th birthday of Takase Seiken, Professor at Kyoto Imperial University. As such, his friends and students have conspired to gather thirty different scholars to author essays from their own field of study."

For many centuries in Japan, particularly during the Edo Period (1600–1864), Confucianism (*jugaku* 儒学), or rather Zhu Xi's Neo-Confucianism, stood as the orthodox philosophical tradition. It was the system by which the shogun state justified and explained itself, and the tradition in which the leading scholars and philosophers worked. Other intellectual traditions, including Buddhism and Shintoism, worked at the margins more often than not defining themselves as the alternative to the dominant Neo-Confucianism. With the Meiji Restoration and Japan's modernization, Neo-Confucianism quickly disappeared as a living philosophy, that is, as something that intellectuals would genuinely believe in and which would frame their thoughts and discussions on the world. By the time Tanabe was a working philosopher, the days of Neo-Confucianism were history, and European philosophy was the only tradition for any serious thinker to be in.

---

1   *Tanabe Hajime Zenshū*, 4:289–301.

Just like with historical-materialism in Eastern Europe before the Berlin Wall came down, Neo-Confucianism had been a self-contained system that could explain everything in its world until that world clashed too much with economic reality, and both world and philosophy collapsed together.

Neo-Confucianism, like any moribund philosophy, will always arouse historical curiosity. It will remain one of the great artifacts of human thinking, a vision of the world that provided meaning and shaped beliefs for many centuries, if not millennia. But the study of alternative philosophies, like the study of alternative religions, also serves as a sharp shock to remind us that our own philosophy and view of life is just one more possible alternative. The beliefs in our head that seem so obvious, the assumptions in our mind that seem such common sense will be odd, quaint, and wrong to others someday. Encountering many faiths can shake one's own but it can also make it humbler, wider, more tolerant, and hence stronger. Some may argue that the study of extinct or dormant philosophies is also worthwhile because they have some *relevance* to us today. Capitalism has its contradictions, as the historical-materialists warned us, and particle physics breaks the rules of essentializing metaphysics, as the Confucianists would have probably foreseen. But granting relevance posthumously to a philosophy can have shades of shallow condescension. We agree with them only because, ultimately, we have made them agree with us. Often, it is better to just enjoy ideas for their own sake and not seek contrived pragmatic justifications for doing so.[2]

In the present essay, Tanabe explores the cosmology of Confucianism through a reading of the *I-Ching*, one of the official five classics of Ancient China. Tanabe focusses on the *Great Commentary*, which, as its name implies, is an appendix to the *I-Ching*, providing the reader with an interpretation main text that very much lays out a coherent cosmological system. What interests Tanabe most is the contrast

---

2   I am aware, of course, that the Chinese speaking world has seen an active New Confucianism tradition emerge in the 20th Century. Indeed, the influential and omnipresent modern Japanese philosopher, Watsuji Tetsurō, laced his writings on ethics with many a Confucian concept. And meanwhile, way over on the other continental tradition, Marxism has long ago been rebooted and turbocharged. But still, never a repeat shall a reboot be, aye.

between the cosmology presented in the *I-Ching* and that of Ancient Greece and of the Judeo-Christian world. Ancient Greek cosmology, in the guise of Aristotle, sees everything as composed essentially of form and matter. But neither form nor matter can exist independently of each other. One always *shapes* the other, we can say. This is a fairly commonsense uncontroversial view of the world. However, the contrasting *I-Ching* view is to see two alternative forces operative in the world: *yin* and *yang*. Unlike form and matter, *yin* and *yang* do not just sit there in the shape of completed objects for the enjoyment of our gaze, instead they are both, in a sense, almost mutually separate forces that are working with and against each other ensuring that our universe is always changing and never stable. The *I-Ching* also clashes with the Judeo-Christian view where God and Satan are in conflict, but with God having always already won. Instead, the *I-Ching* posits a Great ultimate that is not in conflict with anything but is simply just there. The three cosmologies may disagree but each of them does explain everything with a model of the cosmos that works.

Tanabe links the *I-Ching* cosmology to the *Weltanschauung* of farmers (the majority experience for ancient Chinese) and the Aristotelian view to that of classical sculptors. This historical analysis may be potted, and perhaps potty, but it does highlight how the *yin-yang* view does mirror a stark nature view, a world with constant but cyclical growth and decay with no obvious final teleology. On the question of whether the ancient *I-Ching* has any relevance for us today, Tanabe mercifully avoids any superficial platitudes and simply remarks that, of the three cosmologies, the *I-Ching* comes closest to the dialectics of modern philosophy. Praise, indeed, from a continental philosopher of Tanabe's stature.

On Confucianist Ontology

1.

There are many issues concerning the origins of the I-Ching (Book of Changes) and its connection to Confucianism. I will not go into these but either way, for the Confucianism that we have today, it is the ontologie (Ontologie) of the I-Ching 易経 that provides its basic metaphysics. In this way, I hope to look at the broader ontology of Confucianism using clues from the I-Ching. The main text of the I-Ching is exceedingly obscure and a great volume of books seeking to interpret it have been written since ancient times. I am no specialist and my discussion may come across as jejune. My musings on the ontology of the I-Ching shall be garnered from the *Great Commentary*[3], a text which, fortunately for us, gives us the grounds from which a philosophy of the I-Ching may be harvested. I do apologize in advance for my lack of knowledge of Confucianism, any errors I may fall into, and for the possibility that my ideas may be staid and old-fashioned, rather than the innovative insights I hope for.

The Great Commentary tells us that the ancient sages observed the changing events between heaven and earth—the motions of the sun and the moon, the variance of hot and cold, the changes of night and day, the flourishing of nature, life giving way to death—and reduced these to the ebb and flow of two principles: *yin* and *yang*. From this the I-Ching was created. The two divination lines (二卦) of *yin* and *yang* are grounded in this dual principle. They are combined and intwined to express, numerically, the movement and change in all phenomena. Through this medium, we have the eluci-

---

3   The Great Commentary [繋辞伝] is a latter commentary and interpretation of the main part of the I-Ching. It is now seen as an essential appendix to the work.

dation of human morality, the illumination of reason, and the incandescence of spirit, and with this a striven harmony with destiny. The motivation for compiling the I-Ching derived both from metaphysical insights and practical norms. It did not seek out of simple theoretical curiosity the principles governing the evolution and existence of humans in nature, nor did it have a pragmatic agenda to alter the rules of human behavior. It was on the whole focused on these rules but looking at moral standards of human behavior entailed a call for conformity with the rule of heaven, which then automatically involved a search for the principles of actual existence.

What, then, are *yin* and *yang*? We can surmise that they are the principles of flowing-flourishing-motion and retracting-retreating-stillness—the principles manifest in the oppositions between heaven and earth, day and night, light and dark, spring and autumn, summer and winter, man and woman, etc. Quite simply, it is the opposition between the active and the passive. The conjointment of both principles structures our entire actual reality. Now, this conjoining is not simply *yin* and *yang* in equal proportions, but is a complex combination of sixty-four hexagrams (卦) and three hundred and eight-four strokes (爻) based on the joining of the heaven *qian* (乾) and earth *kun* (坤) hexagrams. This *Zahlensymbolik* (numerology) is really the result of searching for concrete symbols that can properly express the formation and changes of actual material reality (現実事物). As such, the I-Ching seeks the unchanging principles underlying changes in the infinite material. A metaphysics to symbolize these changes is established through calculations of the proportions by which these underlying principles mutually wax and wane. It is impossible to symbolize all truths individually as there is infinite complexity as the number of strokes and hexagrams increase. We can only apportion symbols to a limited number of cases. However, by connecting with the Great Commentary which suitably expresses the determination of events through equivalent concretization, the symbols can escape somewhat universal abstraction and connect to the concrete. We can say that the I-Ching is in accordance with heaven and earth, and so therefore embraces the way of heaven and earth. And so a finite number of patterns are arrayed upon real events that change and move forever in complexity and diversity. With this numerology and the Great Commentary to hand, it is possible to determine in principle and predict in practice the arising of events, and to alter our behavior so as to give rise to such events, all by clarifying structures created through the combination of the *yin* and *yang* of existence. This is the reason why the I-Ching is based on the method of divination and at the same time models of morality. However, what are these *yin* and *yang*, which are placed in the grounds for the compilation of the I-Ching? This is never clearly explained. Of course, they are the two opposing principles of activity and passivity. However, in what sense are they opposed? This is not made obvious. Logical affirmation and negation are one type of opposition. So too are the spatial oppositions between north and south, or up and down. Objects and forces also oppose and offset each other through centrifugal and centripetal forces. God and Satan, reason and feelings, these too are oppositions. Internal conflicts of the heart, as in love and hate, are also oppositions. Furthermore, matter and form, material and shape, can be seen, in a sense as active and passive oppositions. Opposing heaven to earth, light to darkness, male to female simply constitute archetypal expressions. It tells us nothing of the actual nature of *yin–yang* duality. If we can be clear about the nature of this opposition, we will be able to know the structure of the ontology in the I-Ching and in Confucianism in general. It will also let us speculate somewhat on the characteristics of the Chinese folk-experiences that gave rise to such an ontology, and what their character and way of life were. Judging the correctness of each interpretation of the Great Commentary in its systemization and explanations of the hexagrams and strokes is not easily done and this presents a problem. This is evident from all the different conflicting interpretations of the I-Ching, going so far as the outlandish *theosophische kosmologie* (theosophical cosmology) fantasies propounded in many quarters. However, a prior and deeper problem in understanding the I-Ching is what exactly this opposition between the principles of *yin* and *yang* elucidates for us. It is this question that I wish to deal with here.

2.

The motivation for creating the I-Ching and the intentions of the authors can be summarized as seeking to reduce the pluralities and changes in the world to a simple unity of unchanging principles. This is the usual common starting point in human speculation. Humans seek a conceptual form of thinking that can anticipate what will happen when one goes about negotiating with the outside world. With this, there emerges a unifying notion that conceptually embraces universal sameness in similar events regardless of particular variations. This need to govern behavior by predicting its consequences, does not simply lead to the comprehensive categorizing of our reality, but spawns reflective thinking on how our deductive explanations of the various types of events that arise are connected to cause-effect relations. The need to know the origins of creation and the ultimate causes of its emergence, and the need to secure universal conceptualizations are both connected in the attempt to reduce to simple and universal principles of super-phenomenal metaphysics the diversity of reality with its boundless change and diversity—the launching point of metaphysical reflectiveness common to all nations—which cannot be directly discovered in reality as it is. Naturally, these principles are to be reduced to a unity in accordance with the requirements for universalizing speculative thought. It is what is called the "great ultimate" (大極). As the I-Ching tells us:

> The I-Ching contains this great ultimate. It gives rise to the two forms. These give rise to the four symbols. The four symbols give rise to the eight hexagrams. [易有太極,是生兩儀,兩儀生四象,四象生八卦]

However, even though there is a necessary reduction here of principles to one dimension, in accordance with the requirements for universalizing speculative thought, these principles—derived as they are, as I have said, by the emergence of the speculative thinking—need to explain the emergence of reality with all its change and diversity. They are not principles if they cannot fulfill this purpose.

Now we must ask: is it possible to derive diversity and change from a simple, singular, unchanging, unmoving principle? Many will instantly say it is not. Metaphysical reflection is spurred by two demands: finding the simplest universal oppositional principles, and explaining actual change and diversity through their interplay. If two polar principles are conceived as being relative opposites relative to the absolute then they are simply mere opposites, and cannot ground the emergence of diversity and change. For this to happen, the polar opposites must be able to link to one another. If they are merely standing opposite to one another and no common mediation exist between them, they cannot enter into a unifying interrelation through themselves. Such an interlinking would only be possible through the mediation of a common universal of which these polarities are seen to be its division. That is to say, a unity, even if it was originally a duality, cannot get us to change and diversity. The ultimate theory that explains change and diversity must include one that will include two as its own differentiation, and two as that which is mediated through the one. To put it another way, it must be three that combines one and two in this sense. This is the reason why the I-Ching (易), which emerges from the great ultimate (大極) stands as the ultimate principle of the duality of *yin* and *yang*, which are united by the great ultimate.

However, in what kind of relationship does the great ultimate unify *yin* and *yang*? And in what kind of relationship is *yin* and *yang* differentiated from and through the great ultimate? As I have just stated, if it is possible to have a theory explaining the endless diversity and change starting with two mediated by one, where one includes the two, then we are not allowed to ask the question of how or why the *yin-yang* of the great ultimate emerges. If we consider it meaningless to ask why there is reality, then it is equally meaningless to ask why there has to be a system of two united in one, which ought to explain the origins of reality. If a theory can be the principle that ground complex diversity and changeable becoming both with the "great ultimate" (where *yin* and *yang* emerges) and the *yin*-and-*yang* (which is unified through the mediation of the Great ultimate), it cannot be meaningful to ask why the great ultimate generates *yin* and *yang*, or why the *yin* and *yang* are mediated by the great ultimate. But we can ask "how" (namely the pattern by which) this happens, as distinct from "why." Doing so will helps us to know the distinct ontology of the I-Ching. If that is the case, then how does the great

ultimate generate the *yin-yang*, and how is the *yin-yang* mediated by
the great ultimate? The Great Commentary's answer to the question
is not at all satisfactory. We get no detailed statements from it, only
metaphorical and symbolic language that hint at its meaning. With
the overburden of citations and similes, the only method left open to
us is to offer conjectures on the relationship between the *yin-yang* and
the great ultimate, the source and mediator of the *yin-yang*, by specu-
lating on the dual opposition of the *yin* and *yang*, the true meaning of
which has been obscured.

So, what kind of principle is the duality of the relatively opposed
yin-yang? *Yang* at its purest is *qiam*, *yin* at its purest is *kun*. The Great
Commentary, in remarks on the *qian-kun* of the *great yin* and *great
yang*, tells us that :

> *qian* is heaven and therefore called father, *kun* is earth, and therefore called
> mother. Heaven is honored, earth is base, *qian* and *kun* are so designated, lowly
> and high are displayed, noble and vulgar have their place, motion and stillness
> are regulated, hardness and softness divided, the *qiam* way of the male is formed,
> the *kun* way of the female is formed, the *qiam* knows the great origination, *kun*
> creates the living.

> 天尊地卑,乾坤定矣。卑高以陳,貴賤位矣。動靜有常,剛柔斷矣。方以類聚,物以群分,吉
> 凶生矣。在天成象,在地成形,變化見矣。是故,剛柔相摩,八卦相盪。鼓之以雷霆,潤之以
> 風雨,日月運行,一寒一暑,乾道成男,坤道成女。乾知大始,坤作成物

With these words we can observe the following: The creation of
life and the world in the I-Ching can be seen as replicating the growth
of plants, trees, fruits, and grains through the heavenly climate and
earthly materials. This compares to the biological fact of sexual repro-
duction most manifest in the reproductive life of men and women.
As such, the *qiam* and *kun*, and the opposition between *yin* and *yang*,
are the opposition between *qi* (氣) and matter, amounting to nothing
more than the opposition between the principles of unfolding movement and contained stillness which supplies the raw stuff (素地) for
that movement. *Kun*, or *yin*, is the foundation upon which growth
occurs, the raw stuff fueling dynamic power.

However, this raw stuff does not have the same ontological meaning as that of matter in Greek ontology which is a principle endowed
with potential but lacking in self-essence, such as to be seen at the

apogee of Aristotelian philosophy. Rather, this raw stuff is following a principle that has its own earthly, motherly, soft, lowly essence. Furthermore, this principle of opposition and conflict with the other on the basis of one's own essence, even with the possession of this essence, is not like the principle of "evil" in Hebrew and Christian ontology. Instead, the generative power of *qian*, or *yang*, whilst having the power to oppose and compete, the same as God with "evil", and even though it may final prevail as such, it is not a power that engages in conflict as in antagonistic combat. The strong and high, through their essence, shall reign everywhere over the weak and the lowly which are naturally their opposite. This action powers the realization of essence. However, unlike in Greek ontology, this does not entail the imprinting of form on matter, nor the movement from latent to manifest as in the particular formation of matter lacking essence.

Qian or *yang* is the dynamic power for continuous evolution, it is not simply form. It is the generating power behind the growth of all living creation. The great ultimate is the motive behind the release of this generative power. Its release anticipates the *yin* as raw stuff, and so the *yang* rather than submitting to a dualistic opposition, takes in the binary *yin-yang* into itself, and is observed as the movement not yet moving, the power not yet released. This Great ultimate is the base one-dimensional original *qi* (元氣) that is the grounds for the generation of Creation. In the emergence of life, in actual reality, though, the *yang* as the generating flow of the original *qi*, and the *yin*, its raw stuff, are separate. All the different things in creation are merely the waxing and waning of the opposing *yin* and *yang*. This idea of a Great ultimate as a base one-dimension splitting into a relative two should not be seen as equivalent to the opposition between form and matter in Greek ontology or between God and "evil" in Christian ontology. In Greek ontology, matter is the principle of potentiality without essence, and form is latent in this. There is a link and unity between both from the very start and so no one-dimension as mediator is needed. Although, of course, as readers of Greek philosophy know, before Aristotle, Plato did problematize this issue of mediation.

In Hebraic and Christian ontology, on the other hand, where "evil" is seen as a degradation within God, Satan, as the principle of "evil" and sin, is not directly opposed to God but rather, at all times,

subservient to Him. So, again, there is no need for a mediator trans-
cendent of the opposition between the two. However, looking at the
theories of freewill seen in Augustine at the beginning of Christianity, through Boehme, and onto Schilling in the 18th Century, whenever the origins of "evil" are examined, and its autonomy emphasized,
up sprouts the problem of God's immanence and sin due to freewill.
Let us acknowledge, anyway, this dualist oneness in the theory of the
I-Ching and how it stands in contrast to these other latent and imma-
nent dualisms, in that from the beginning it clearly extols the dialectic structure of existence. In the I-Ching, the movement of the great
ultimate is *yang*, and the raw stuff for this is *yin*. Both *yin* and *yang*
are of the great ultimate. The great ultimate splits, and we get the *yin*
and the *yang*. Now, when the power of the original *qi* of the great ultimate generates it becomes *yang*. This means the great ultimate is *yang*
that has not generated yet. However, the *yin* in its opposition to the
yang has no powers of negation. It is always the principle of passivity
that is soft and inferior providing the raw stuff for the movement of
the *yang*, and so even though it is opposite to the *yang*, it is never in
conflict with it, it is always meekly following the *yang*, accepting its
movement.

In this way, the great ultimate, with its yet to be generated *yang*, will
include the *yin*. This makes it different to God which does not contain "evil" within Himself but rather "evil" is included as something
that resists Him. By contrast, the inclusion of the *yin* is the mediation of reality itself in complete submission to itself. To be generating implies that movement moves from the beginning in opposition
to stillness. This means that movement is always becoming through
the raw stuff in its stillness, and stillness exists as the mediation of
movement. This splitting of the great ultimate into *yin* and *yang* is its
coming into motion through the mediation of stillness. *Yin*, in this
sense, is the Great ultimate's tendency towards stillness, and *yang* is
its dynamic side. When the Original *Qi* emerges from the Great ultimate as *yang*, there must always be that which does not move, but
remains still, acting as the mediator, identifying the movement of that
which moves. This is the *yin*. The opposition between *yin* and *yang* is
quite simply this conceptual opposition. *Yin* is not, as such, in reality,

opposed, as in resisting, the movement of the *yang*. There is no resisting power that could hinder or oppose the power of the *yang*.

The *yang* will always need a non-mover that is opposite it conceptually so that the *yang*'s movement can appear and be recognized as movement. The *yang* is identified as *yang* through this conceptual opposition. As it is of the Great ultimate, it is generated entirely by the Great ultimate, as the mediator for the *yang* to appear. The splitting of the Great ultimate into *yin* and *yang* means that the Great ultimate divides and is split into two genuinely opposing forces. This means that conflict is not born within the Great ultimate. Rather, it is the movement that arises from the Great ultimate, and the still, unmoving *yin*, the opposition to that *yang* movement, which appears opposite the *yang* as the mediator differentiating and manifesting it. With such movement, the Great ultimate manifests the movement in one aspect, and manifests the stillness aligned to that movement as another aspect. A stilled movement is not movement, and unmoving stillness is not stillness. Movement needs stillness to be movement, and stillness needs movement to be stillness. The great ultimate is not movement or stillness, and at the same time it is pure movement and pure stillness. In this way, *yin* is conceptually opposed to *yang* as its mediator manifesting *yang*. It has no active power to resist in reality but, unlike matter in Greek ontology, it is not at all lacking in self-essence. It absorbs the strong and lofty power of the *yang*, and supplies the raw stuff with which the *yang* operates. But with this, it is a passive being that possesses its own essence that is of the soft and lowly. It is not simply a contradictory contentless opposition for theoretical negation, but is, conceptually, a resisting opposition that has its own determination.

If we connect matter, the passive principle in Greek ontology, to theoretical negation on account of it having no self-essence, and call this the *contradicting* opponent, then "evil", the passive principle in Hebraic-Christian ontology, should be called the *realistic* conflicting opponent. In contrast to these, the *yin*, the passive principle in Confucian ontology, must be understood as the *conceptually* resisting opponent coming somewhere in-between both. Let us think about the dialectics of thesis-antithesis-synthesis whereby there is a unity of two as one. Dialectics emerges with the concretization of resisting oppositions that arise from the simple theoretical negation of the thesis by it's antithesis. The concept of the Great ultimate allows for the I-Ching's ontology to express a much clearer dialectic unity when compared to the other two (Greek and Christian) ontologies. It ought to be admired for this. The dividing opposition of the *yin* and *yang* of the Great ultimate in the I-Ching can be seen as having this structure.

3.

If there are no great errors in my analysis above of the ontology of the I-Ching, then we can surmise to some extent the historical special features of the ethnic consciousness that gave development to such an ontology. This form of ontology is linked to basic experiences of growth and generation. In this connection I have compared the I-Ching's view of generation to that found in the ontologies of Greece and Christianity. The opposition of *yin* and *yang* is the ultimate principle of opposition in the I-Ching's ontology. This is not the same as the theoretical negation found in the contradictory opposition between form and matter, such as in Greek ontology, nor is it the real conflictual opposition to be found between God and "evil" in Judeo-Christian ontology. Instead it is a conceptual opposition that can be conceived as lying between both Greek and Judeo-Christian ontologies. To repeat the point, *yin* is different to the Greek notion of matter in that matter is merely potential and does not have self-essence, whereas *yin* is always existing in opposition to *yang* with its own self-essence. When these two opposing principles with their own self-essence meet in reality and negotiate with one another through opposition, the question naturally emerges as to whether this is the same as the opposition in reality that is seen in Hebrew ontology, or does it simply mean theoretical opposition?

Things can exist in reality in opposition to one another without this implying real conflict in terms of power relations. This is possible when theoretically one is in opposition to the other's existence through a mediating relationship. When things are directly opposed to one another in reality, one establishes itself by reducing the other.

At the very least, it establishes itself by overcoming the other through the power of its own self which is a power that can never be in conflict with itself by becoming the other. Also, theoretical opposition involves a mediation which will always need the other regardless of whether one is in conflict with that other. One and another can coexist in a structure where both are arrayed together, without one conquering the other. Theoretical opposition is that which allows for a single structure wherein two can coexist. This is not simply the bare fact of two standing merely opposite one another but is an opposition that appears from the beginning from a self-reflectiveness in the structure where both one and the other dwell. In sum, we are looking at opposition in reality being projected onto opposition in theory. It is the opposition of *yin* and *yang* that conforms most completely to this kind of opposition. Accordingly, it is an opposition to be found in a relationship where one side is leading and the other following. It is not an opposition residing in unstructured conflict born of resistance, but is a conflict build on a descant relationship of one leading, one following, within a structure. This opposition is not the clash of power to be found in actual conflicts but is the essential opposition between two things in an equal order, the theoretically qualitative opposition of such contrastive polarities.

The *yin-yang* seeks its model in the opposition between male and female, between husband and wife, between heaven and earth, between master and servant. These are binary opposites that are in reality in mutual conflict but are endowed with a structural harmony. They must be conceptualized and projected onto a theoretical opposition where one is in reality the grounds for the mediation of the other. This consciousness, formed as it is from the polarities found in general existence shaped by dual principles governing such a structured opposition, when taken to be the basic experience to be found in all our experiences, becomes the empirical model for the moral and social structure, and the political consciousness of the so called sage ruler.

As I have said, the creation of the I-Ching was not motivated by the search for theoretical knowledge. Rather, it was to harmonize morality, the standards of human behavior, with the Way of Heaven. And with this, find means for human nature to reach its full potential. Morality, at the daily level, follows the Way of Heaven in its flow. Accordingly, the morality of the people submits to the ruler who represents this Way of Heaven. The I-Ching was compiled through observations of the movements of the heavens and nature. The consciousness behind these observations was a moral consciousness filled with the basic experiences of having structures dividing the ruler and the ruled, and the relationship between the commands of the ruler and the obedience of the ruled. Observing the structures in the movements of nature, it was possible to discern the grounds for the waxing and waning of the *yin* and *yang*. Without this, it would be impossible to see what is behind the incessant conflicts between these powers in nature. We could not know the actual ultimate grounds upon which lurk these two principles opposed in reality. Ontology is the interpretation of existence by itself. So, its answers will always reflect models of visible existence and patterns of life. The ontology of the I-Ching is the womb for moral consciousness birthed into the structure of society. Focusing on these origins, we can naturally see its usefulness for further reflections on the metaphysical foundations of morality.

We can see here the connection with and comparison to Confucian morality. The work of farmers, governed by the change of the season and the course of the weather, is the teacher of moral government. This privileging of the agrarian we can take to have been of a time when the lifestyle of the people who gave birth to this ontology was tethered to the labor of the soil. The moral consciousness of a ruling class aiming to righteously govern according to the social structures of a people immersed in the toil of agriculture no doubt pondered and reflected on the experiences of such an existence, with the ontology of the I-Ching being the fruits of this hunt for metaphysical principles. This relationship between the ontology of the I-Ching and the shape of the ethnic consciousness that molded it is clear when we make a comparison with the other Greek and Judeo-Christian ontologies.

The duality of Greek ontology, as in the opposition between form and matter in Aristotle, does not prevent talk of final completion. Matter is potential without self-essence. For reality to be the various different things that it is, matter links with form, making it what it is: eidos. We can explain this way of thinking with an analogy from art: the relationship between the material from which a statue is made and the manner in which it is formed. The Greek, aroused by the spirit that shapes nature, looked at all existence with the eyes of a sculptor, seeing it as the shaping of matter and the imitation of sculpted form. In this sense, Greek ontology is archetypically artistic, mostly seeking to understand all existence from a standpoint of symbolic reflection. They shirked unstable confusion and shunned the infinite for its endlessness. Their view of existence, where the world is elegantly symbolized as spheres in perfect harmony and determinateness, was an artistic one.

Judeo-Christian ontology contrasts with this featuring as it does a conflict between infinite God and "evil" which resists Him. Here, instead of the complete formation through resplendent harmony as with the Greeks, we see the vestiges of conflict and resistance within a determined infinite. Existence manifests the different stages in this conflict between God and Satan. This viewpoint is religious, and mostly corresponds to a model of human will and experience. Both of these worldviews are extremely conflictual offering models of symmetrical opposition.

By contrast, Confucian ontology has a passive principle which has its own self-essence. Furthermore, even with this self-essence, it submits without resistance to the active principle. Instead of letting itself be formed, it progresses through its own nature, mediating in the realization of movement and the development of the active principle. It is submission without resistance according to a structure. This clearly can be called an ethical ontology, as distinct from an artistic or religious one. It can also be described as a sentimental ontology in contrast to a symbolic or willed one. This is because the core of Confucianist ethics is a virtue ethics and not a rational ethics (ethic of goodness) like in Kantian ethics. Goodness comes from a particular structure of the will whereas ethics derives from sentiment that is born of a socially conditioned state of mind.

I believe that the three models of ontology can be characterized thus: Greek ontology is a symbolic model based on artistic experience; Judeo-Christian ontology is a human will model based on religious experience. And Confucian ontology is a sentiment model arising from the empirical ethics of which the sage rulers were endowed.

As I have said before, and do not need to explain again, the third model tends to come between the first and the second.

The above crude investigation has been following an analysis of the ontology of the I-Ching. However, it has also involved speculation on the ethnic spirit and experience, as well as cultural conditions, that gave rise to this ontology. It is not in my power nor is it my place to confirm or disagree with actual scholarship in cultural history. I have, needless to say, through my studies become aware of how much further I must think about these matters.

KIMURA MOTOMORI

THE FORM OF BEAUTY

Translated by Takeshi Morisato, with Kyle Michael James Shuttleworth

Chapter 1
Form and Ideal

1. *Introducing a problem*

Rhetoric is an art. However, we do not call a simple, daily conversation an art. Whereas poetry is an art. Language (言葉), when it is spoken poetically, undergoes a series of transformations through rhythm. But rhythm is the form that time has. When it loses this form, poetry breaks down and the language will fall apart like flowerpetals in the wind. According to Alain, poetry "follows the law of time" and rhetoric "thinks under the law of time" and the form of a story is the "time that has passed."[1] He further argues that "harmony (*nombre*, 諧調) has already determined an empty form and words come to occupy their positions therein," and that the balanced correspondence between many words and "rhythmical movement" (律動) finally secures this harmony (諧調).[2] Various determinations of time were also the scheme of the concept of pure understanding in Kant. The trans-temporal meaning could come forth to the real world only by being connected to various forms of time and then by supporting the experience from its ground. The significance of the form of time

---

1   [Alain is the pseudonym of Émile-Auguste Chartier (1868–1951), a French philosopher who had a major influence on the 20th century Francophone philosophy along with Henri Bergson and Paul Valéry. His *Propos sur le bonheur* (1928) is his most famous work in Japan, but Kimura is referring to Kuwabara Takeo's (1904–1988) Japanese translation, 幸福論.]

2   See Kuwabara Takeo's translation of 散文論.

that it has in the world of knowledge as a scheme is incomparable with the richness of the meanings that various forms of time have in the world of art. Many words (言葉) in their wild-dance correspond to various forms of time which constitutes their marvelous marriage; and from there, poetry is born. This is not only about poetry. Nor is it only about rhetoric or stories. The art of language (言葉) cannot be established at all unless it is tied to some form of time. Prose also has a style. I am certain that it takes the "breaking out of tune," which is like "walking around a place with terrible footing" as its essential character. Nevertheless, we do not think that this would reject a peculiar style from superior prose as a guest who should not be invited. The style, the taste (風格), so on and so forth, insofar as they appear in the art of language (言葉), cannot be seen as that which can be established apart from any form of time. When apart from time, prose cannot express itself as a good artwork even though it may be able to at least transmit the meaning that it tries to convey to a reader.

Now, we could think of the "already empty form" of time as that which stands in opposition to the words (言葉) apart from them. However, should we be able to say that this form, as that which is empty beforehand, stands over against that which comes out of the words, namely the content that enters into the form of time in language? Here the problem must become profound for us. This reminds me of Goethe's *Der Erlkönig* (The Erlking). Could we think about the rhythm of that poem as that which has already existed as form, which could absorb other poems, prior to the content that the poet recites to conjure and bring forth with language? The form of *tanka*, the form of *haiku*, seven-five rhythm, and three-five rhythm—indeed, we already have an established form of poetry in Japan. In this manner, we choose the words and insert them. However, would every artistic meaning, which emerges in language, meekly affirm its voluntary insertion into these pre-established forms? It is difficult to think in this way. The content requires a certain form in accordance with its nature. Some necessarily require the seven-five rhythm, and others the three-five. Indeed, form is universal; and content is individual and because of that it can enter into the form—tentatively, we should be able to think [about the relation of form and content] in this way. Moreover, a more profound problem remains at the foundation. As the content chooses the form, putting it the other way around, a single form, even if it can accept a certain content, cannot continue penetrating other contents. —What does this say to us? I wonder whether this could be a warning: the way of thinking that takes the content and the form as that which oppose each other, this idea itself is not truly fundamental.

The art of language cannot be separated from the form of time. Without a doubt, this point appears most prominently in poetry. This fact is even more evident in vocal music. Perhaps poetry is not only to be just read, but also to be spontaneously read out loud and eventually to be sung. When the content, emerging from language, tries to claim its meaning through entwining the sound of words and the form of time, there is a transition (移り行き) from poetry to vocal music, or more generally speaking, a transformation from the art of language to the art of sound. The meaning is hidden inside the embrace between time and the sound of words: that is where the art of singing (歌う芸術) is established. When divorced from that form, it has to be exiled from the country of the art of singing. However, sound, in one sense, gives a body of meaning that emerges from language and further the clothing that covers it, and at the same time independently claims its own meaning entirely apart from (the concept of) language. Accordingly, it can display the meaning that we cannot convey through language, the meaning that exhausts words, goes beyond language, and transcends it both in height and depth. Moreover, the independent sound, whether it is in and for itself, or in a whole that is relevant to it—through an unknown series of secret rites—mysteriously becomes united with the spirit of color and sound, and thereby places its incredible heart-and-mind (心) into a communicative relation with spatial form (形象) and other natural objects—even if we choose simple examples, they include yellow, bright, round, sharp, rusty voices, etc. The metallic line and other strings, various pipes and elastic surfaces, further allow the function of the vocal chords to transcend themselves in a certain direction. Namely, the self-transcendence of vocal chords towards musical instruments. Here, all matter (matière) demonstrates its unique tone (音色). The world of sound is thus materially expanded and enriched. —A simple sound is not only tied to feelings, as we would say about a sad voice or a pleasant sound, but also tied to light, color, and a variety of spatial forms in this manner, which further demonstrates the diverse meanings which transcend language both in depth and height. From here, when sounds become independent, and as each of them are interrelated with the other, and when they become united and harmonized with the form of time in their mutual necessity, the particularly superior and symbolic world of art is unfurled. Melody in particular is a wonderful and beautiful child born in such a world. If we think about the trans-conceptual height and depth of sound, Schopenhauer was perhaps right about placing music at the highest stage of art as he clarified its symbolic nature in his *Die Welt als Wille und Vorstellung* (The World and Will and Representation). Once again, we can say this: when the continuity of sound is insulated from the form of time, it does not deserve the honor of art in any sense. Only chaotic noise dominates therein.

Now, as sound goes on streaming in diverse forms through time—sometimes lightly like rolling a ball, sometimes like tumbling water, sometimes like a storm or a broad stream full of water, or the crashing of surging waves—when the form of space flows inside time through various transformations (変転), what is revealed therein is the world of dance. That is, the fantastic and pure union of the spatial form (形象) and the form (形) of time. The shape (形姿) of a human body streams into the rhythm of time. The coagulated nature of space is being melted into the fluidity of time. We could say that dance is the music of the spatial form. That is to say, sound is changed into a pure form (形象) therein. Language is not allowed to enter here. The symbolic nature of dance, just like music, is based on this point. The flow (流動) of time shapes the stream (流れ) of symbols by melting all forms (形象). However, at the bottom of this flow of time, which constantly streams to and fro without knowing how to stop itself, is time in which space recovers its coagulability (凝結性), and thereby, the continuity of time is momentarily torn, which gives birth to crystalized styles (姿態) in *Noh* and *Kabuki*. It is not a mere negation of endlessly streaming life towards static death, but rather a crystallization of life at a higher level, which instantly sublates the stream in its entirety; it is the eternal present (永遠の現在) that transcends the flow of time. As the sea with constantly moving waves symbolically crystalizes an amazing shape of a wave that leaps up in a moment to the eye of the beholder, when the space that is melted inside time reaches the limit of its height or depth in its rhythmical motion, it leaps out of the stream from the streambed and shows the meaning of the stream at the higher, momentary pause that denies time. Hence, we do not say that the next movement rises beyond it. Instead, it emerges as it streams downwards from [the higher point of pause]. Perhaps, a good sculpture is also about grasping a still of dynamic life in this sense?

As sound transitions from vocal music to pure music by departing from the meaning of language, when space that is tied to time as the form (形象) of music moves in the reverse direction of recovering language, what appears here at first is probably the transition from dance to opera. This direction, as it sublates the form of time, continues to progress into the elevation of spatiality. That which has still more recovered the linguistic meaning or, nay, that which has completely retrieved it, this is where drama is established. [This is where] the stream of time continues to lose its power and the form of space becomes more and more dominant. Accordingly, language that can originally and, in reality, only exist in time also becomes locked into the silence of space. Time coagulates and crystalizes inside space; and in profound silence, a world is revealed. We discovered therein the world of plastic arts (造形美術). Rodin's *The Thinker* never opens his mouth. Da Vinci's "Mona Lisa" sends the infinite smile that has no words beyond the rhythm of time. Some have dared to say and show us that "architecture is crystalized music."

We have thus far followed this line of thinking: if what governs the whole process from the art of language to that of sound through vocal music is the form of time, then how can the formality (形式) of time coagulate itself in space, which gradually heightens its dominance, while being bound to the form of space? If we trace this in reverse order, the meaning coagulated in real (実在的) space begins to flow as it is gradually dissolved into the stream of time, rises to the surge of temporality, and its ebbing tide gradually retreats inside the ideal (観念的) space. The meaning in plastic art that is crystalized in real space develops itself on the one hand as the form of movement by gaining temporality, and on the other hand it simultaneously gains phrases

(文節) through the form of time, thereby turning into language. The synthesis of the developments in these two sides constitutes a drama. Moreover, it progresses from here to an opera in accordance with the development of temporality's positive control; and temporality further affirms itself and progresses to the symbolic nature of dance by taking music, which allows linguality (言語性) to be completely consumed in the form of pure time itself, as its partner. Space is completely dissolved inside time and the world of pure music is revealed; and thereby, space that is sublated in time loses its reality and, as we say, "round sound" or "deep sound" maintains its symbolic nature simply as an ideal in sound alone. If dance is the music of form, music is probably the dance of time. The symbol that has gone beyond and departed from linguistic meaning once again comes down to the lower linguistic sphere from that height. This is where the level of vocal music is developed and time is gradually sunk into the entanglement of conceptual meaning. From poetry further to prose: even in this direction, perhaps, space has not completely vanished. Generally speaking, that which is spatial is left as it is, as that which is ideal and representational, as Alain for example states "we can always discover the center of perspective in a novel," the spatiality at the base (裾野) of time rather secretly maintains a single power of control as the ideal. The base of time, in this manner, gradually loses its reality in the ideal space. There, we should be able to find the levels pertaining to stories, legends, and essays. Finally, the base completely loses its temporal slope in the plain of ideal space, where mere vocabularies are scattered around.[3]

Of course, this simple observation does not fully grasp or clarify the essence of these arts. For instance, we would have to say that we have overlooked the important essence of drama if we only say that

---

3   We could easily outline in mind the following chart [in relation to this point]. We cannot indeed reduce the relations of various arts into one. I have tried to think about them here in terms of the crossing place (*basho*) of temporality and spatiality. Both sides of the vertical line are real and conceptual space. If we trace from the right to left, the curve of time gradually rises from the world of vocabularies, which is the nontemporal field of ideal space, ideal space, and after entering the area of real space, further goes down and reaches the plastic art and finally, perhaps ends with the complete loss of its own self in the field of mere materials of plastic art. Of course, since the purpose of this chart is to propose a problem, the divisions of various arts remains in a very schematic sketch.

the principle of dance in the unity of time and space, as it is bound to language, moves towards the further emphasis of spatial coagulation. That is because we are not at all giving sufficient consideration to the relation of characters, or namely their personal relations, which constitute the most important moment of drama. Needless to say, monodrama is merely an anormal and abstract form (奇形的抽象形態). However, regardless of that, we would not say that our investigation [into the nature of art] was not entirely unessential even regarding drama. Drama that does not have words (or namely any lines)—in the same way as a silent show would have to be the abstract form of drama—a spatially formless drama that moves in time, namely drama that does not have gestures (所作) is simply a closet drama (*Lese-drama*). We have taken the form (形式) of art as the main theme of our consideration from the beginning. This is precisely the viewpoint from which we have been paying attention to the form of time and space, especially in relation to art. To lose these forms, needless to say, means for each art to lose its form, and to become that which is formless. Dance without rhythm, vocal music without melody: could we possibly understand each of them in its own name? Some may argue that there is also a beauty in that which has a broken form. Moderns have indeed discovered the beauty of "deformity" very well. They would not prevent a broken *Shimada-mage* or *Shimada-kuzushi* from claiming their names in the world of beauty.[4] Nonetheless, the broken form is still a form. In the same way as the unbroken form, there is one positive aspect per broken form. The broken form is still that which has form. Contrariwise, regarding that which is without form, how could it be an art anyway? The *form* (かたち) is originally the way of being for a thing (もの) to appear outside. When losing form, the thing cannot manifest itself outside by itself. When *no form* remains (あとかたもなき), the thing has completely vanished. The thing cannot be expressive at that point. How could we discover art therein?

---

4   [Shimada is a traditional Japanese hairstyle, similar to the European pompadour. The *Shimada-mage* has a bun or topknot (*mage* 髷) at the back of the head, and was popular among the women of samurai families. The Shimada kuzushi, was a "simplification" (*kuzushi* 崩し) of the Shimada, which had a cloth wrapped around the top-knot, and was popular among middle-aged townwomen during the late Edo period.]

However—perhaps we must expect some questions here—why did we only pay attention to the form of time and space? Is this what we call the form of art? I am driven by a great urge to boldly answer that "it is" while deferring an important proviso. People perhaps assume some questions about what pertains to intensive variables (内包量的なもの). For instance, they include the contrast or harmony of color or that of sound, and also conflict of will- and physical-power, their harmony or collaborative relations. Indeed, they are all form as an intensive power relation and it does not essentially have anything to do with the duration that occupies appearance or extensive variables: (for instance, the harmony or contrast that takes place due to the change of density in two colors, e.g. green and brown, that fills two squares of the same size)—however, we have to firstly take a step back and think deeply (about the following). Aren't their various relations, namely form(s), established in "ratio"? Does ratio not govern therein? Is the ratio not precisely the relation of numbers and further, as Kant once said, the determination of time? Leibniz calculated the numbers at the hidden foundation of intensive relations. I am not planning on critiquing these things. However, I would like to simply propose this as a caution. Of course, the intensive ratio in art does not pertain to mathematical understanding (数学的悟性) but must be given in the intuition of imagination (構想力の直感). Also, so long as it is a ratio, does it not have to be essentially connected to the principle of extensive quantity in a profound fashion? Not only that, but also is the ratio of imagination not of quantity but rather of quality, and the mutual proportion between aesthetic meanings of mental images (心像) generated by aesthetic imagination, while the ratio of numbers is, so to speak, the abstraction of such living ratio? This is a conditional sentence proposed as a caution. Secondly, in relation to that which is intensive, I would like to write down the following condition as a promise, which is to say that I will give a positive consideration to it when I talk later about *Materialgerechtigkeit* (truth to materials). Under these conditionals, I would like to bind and maintain the abovementioned statement of "it is" [which is to say, the form of time and space is the form of art]. That is, because time and space are originally the form of sensibility and the form of real existence, which is real in the sense of being concrete. We can hardly think about art that is not an expression. Thus, that which is expressive is necessarily concrete and real existence in time and space as externalized innerness, and needless to say, such a thing is the object of intuition as sensible existence. Whatever is intensively variable, insofar as it claims its civil rights in the world of art, must necessarily maintain its concrete realness in the form of time and space.

Then, if we think in this manner, it is not off the mark to think about the form of art in relation to the form of time and space. So long as art is an expression, it is an external appearance of the internal; and the form is that which is as if it were outside the internal, and must be the way of being (有り様). However, if that is the case, then, in order for us to truly think about the form, we must not take it out simply as such and deal with it as the form, but treat it in its relation to innerness. This is where we must come to see the relation of form and content as the appropriate viewpoint for thinking about the problem of form. I believe we have been able to finish setting forth here the main problem [of this book].

2. *That which seeks form* (形式)

Art is an expression. An expression means that the internal life is made to appear outside. To appear outside is for the inner to become concrete, which precisely means that the inner becomes objective as an object of intuition. Form signifies the principle in which that which is internal is being concrete in this manner. Then what is this inner? In order to investigate the problems concerning the essence of form, the process of its formation, its realization, etc., let us begin dealing with this question.

The inner must mean that its expression gives its concretization. If that is the case, then the inner must be initially that which does not yet have any form. However, this cannot mean that [that which does not yet have any form] has no relativity to the form. That is because the inner of the expressed should originally possess the concreteness of self for the first time outside and accordingly, it would have to be that which has the essential connection to the form. Thus, the formlessness of the inner is not the simple negation of the form, but rather the lack of form. The lack means indigency of what there should be. Hence, it means nothing but the possibility towards form. Here lies the affirmative nature that the formlessness of the inner possesses. To be able to be made into form, plasticity (可塑性) is precisely its character. However, we cannot immediately confuse this with the external material's—for instance marble's—plasticity. The plasticity of expressive innerness precisely means the plasticity that is lived as the internal impulse, or more precisely the endless demand towards form. It is the demand that seeks its completeness, concreteness by escaping what is lacking in itself, which makes itself incomplete and abstract, namely the expressive impulse or the will.

However, even if we think in this way, we cannot say that we have particularly discovered the artistic innerness. That is because the practical will is not satisfied with itself as being merely the determining (決意的) innerness. It not only necessarily demands the concrete and objective manifestation of itself as the active externality (行爲的外), but the intellectual demand of itself as the internal also calls for the objective completion (客観的成態) of knowledge that we can reach; and in this sense, we can ground a reason even in an academic study when we can say it is the expressive product of will towards truth. Intellect (知) in this sense has various studies as the expressive completion of internal demand, in this manner practical will also establishes the world of act (行爲) as its expression, and thereby forms a variety of ethical relations, organizations, institutions, facilities, manners, etc. All of which obviously have some sort of form in each of their ways of being and that which is formed. Hence, if we only make the abovementioned statement, "[it is] an expressive innerness that demands form," we cannot say that we have provided the determinations that particularly characterize the artistic will. Study, morality, and art, each of them as the expression of will towards truth, goodness, and beauty, can be thought *in toto* as the realization of will towards culture as the objective formation of humanity. Then, in a more determinate fashion, what kind of thing, we should think, the inner of art as a culture could be?

If we say expressive innerness, it would have to be internal life that seeks to go out towards expression. In this matter, if not only practice, but also intelligence (知性) in one sense belongs to such internal life, then what would have to be especially the inner of artistic expression? What kind of characteristics do the expressive inner, which especially constitutes beauty, have vis-à-vis truth and goodness? Kant, as it is well known, indicated the essential character of beauty in terms of non-conceptuality and disinterestedness vis-à-vis these two. Beauty does not belong to conceptual knowledge. Aesthetic judgment is not established as the theoretical cognition of object. Nor does beauty as a whole relate to goodness. Goodness can be good because of its use and good for its own sake. The former is pleasant (快適) to us as a means for some end; whereas the latter, namely the moral good, is pleasant in itself. At any rate, what is included here is the concept of purpose and accordingly, pleasure in the object of real existence (現実的存在) or in the act (行為) of real existence. That is to say, in this manner, this signifies nothing other than the fact that interestedness is generally essential to goodness. However, where departed from this interest appears to lie the essence of beauty—Kant's analysis [of beauty] here is outstanding. When we say that "this rose is beautiful," we are not increasing the theoretical cognitive determination of an object through it. Nor is it based on interest in the real existence of object. Generally speaking, the real existence of an object or act is completely irrelevant to beauty itself. Beauty is uncompromisingly appearance (仮象的, *Scheinende*) in relation to realness (実在性) in that sense of the word. Rather, here lies the special realness of beauty. When we discussed the concrete reality (具体的現実性) of artistic expression, its reality (現実性) and objectivity would have to be completely different from that which we have discussed as something to do with the aforementioned interests. We would have to clearly distinguish between realness (実在性) that relates to desire (意欲) and aesthetic realness. —Now because of that, the innerness of artistic expression, insofar as it is the inner that relates to beauty, would always have to be, without exception until the end, that which takes non-conceptuality and disinterestedness as its essential character. However, to deny the concept, and to negate interest in itself still remains a negative determination. What would be the positive content of such a thing? The inner that is neither conceptual nor pertaining to will—it would have to be nothing but feelings (感情). When we talk about feelings in the broad sense, is it always non-conceptual or disinterested in every sense of the word? Can all feelings, as what they are immediately, be the inner of artistic expression? I do not think so. Both intellect and practice pertain to will with regard to their working foundation, if various sexual desires are broadly connected to the surroundings of the practical domain, the fulfillment of these desires would have to be accompanied by and result in various feelings of pleasure, the feelings of satisfaction. However, as it is clearly the case, we cannot say that these feelings are simply in themselves nonconceptual and disinterested. Then, what kind of feelings can be particularly artistic? We have already mentioned non-conceptuality and disinterestedness as the essential characteristics of artistic feelings. If that is the case, then when these two determinations are carried out to the fullest in relation to all feelings, and also when feelings that are accompanied by all conceptual activities and all the movements of desires are rejected as inessential in terms of art, what we can extract from this process would have to appear as that which we have been looking for [as aesthetic feelings]. The non-conceptual and disinterested innerness, in this way, will come to manifest itself vividly. It is the innerness that is cleansed of the muddled mixture of concept and interest in every possible sense of the word and in this sense, it must be precisely *pure feeling* (純粋感情).

Opposed to such pure feeling, where are the intellect and that which pertains to will washed off? Where are they rejected and removed to? Has pure feeling completely discarded these things outside itself? If that is the case, then how could art deal with such an abundant life (豊かなる人生)? For instance, how can ethical relations be the content of art? Pure feeling would have no choice but to become extremely abstract. Additionally, the intellect and that which pertains to will cannot be immediately of art. If we think in this way, the problem clearly lies in the way of negation or the way of washing off.

What kind of negation is it? The outward negation makes the pure feeling step into abstract poverty. What increases the pure feeling towards concrete richness (具体的豊満) is to internally negate the intellect and that which pertains to will. This manner of negation removes abstract purity from feeling and raises it to the level of *concrete purity*. What does it mean, however, to negate inwardly? It must mean precisely to go under the foundation of the intellect and that which pertains to will and then to transcend it (深く超えていく). In opposition to intellect and will, which seek the fulfillment of their demands in the objective direction, in reverse of the noematic direction, that is to say, in the noetic direction, transcending them is to inwardly negate the intellect and the will. Intellect and will that seek their fulfillment in the objective direction immerse themselves in their own activities, that is to say, they are bound by themselves in this manner, drowned in themselves. To trans-descend (底へ超える) these things means to preserve them as what they are and at the same time, further from their profound internal background and the foundation of subject (主体的な底), to wrap them up (包み取る). Here, as they are transcended and negated, they are absolutely affirmed and taken in (摂取されている) from the standpoint in which they are not bound. What is manifested here is the standpoint that purely contemplates these things from their *inside* in an intimate and inseparable togetherness (相即) without being drowned in them. The true significance of the phrase, "washing off," is precisely to purify them from a more profound inside and to assimilate them (摂収する). Here lies the activity of pure feeling. It is not abstractly pure by externally negating and discarding that which pertains to intellect and will, but rather renders itself to be concretely pure by transdescending them in great depth and by internally subsuming them. We can say that the inner of artistic expression in this sense is the absolute affirmation of all content of life.

I do think that Kant has strongly suggested the passage towards this manner of thinking. Beauty is a kind of pleasure and aesthetic judgment is a judgment of feeling. However, unlike the judgment of mere empirical pleasure, it demands universal validity from the subject. How is this possible? One of the most important problems for Kant resided in this question. In other words, it is the problem of the transcendental deduction (先験的演繹) of aesthetic judgment. If aesthetic judgment, as it is judgment based on feeling, can also demand universal validity, feeling itself is not constituted merely by empirical character, but it also has to possess an *a priori* principle (先天的原理) in itself. Kant thought that the *a priori* moment, which constitutes feeling in this manner, so long as it relates to beauty (優美), is understanding and imagination. The former is the theoretical faculty when it works towards the particular through categories, and in that case, imagination also acts towards the particular as the schemata. The knowledge of objects is established through the corporation of such particular activities made by the understanding and the imagination towards the intuitively given. However, in this case, only intellectual judgment is established, but not aesthetic judgment. Thus, contrariwise, when understanding works in the manner of generality (überhaupt), it is the faculty of lawfulness (合法性), and when imagination also works in the same manner of generality, it is the faculty of free play of representation. Now, if these two *a priori* faculties are brought to a harmonious activity through one thing, like a single flower, aesthetic pleasure takes place. In this manner, when imagination "in its freedom" and understanding "in its lawfulness" harmonize and cooperate with each other (*KdU*, 146) and finally establish the "free lawfulness of imagination" (op. cit. 69) in this manner, it precisely forms the *a priori* structure of aesthetic feeling. This is where we discover the ground of the universal validity of aesthetic judgment. Kant thought in this way.

Feeling, for Kant, is established in this way as it takes the direct unity of two *a priori* operations (作用) as its constitutive principle. It seems that we would here have to acknowledge the high-dimensionality (高次性) and autonomy of feeling. In this case, regardless of the fact that imagination in its theoretical use as that which is "blind" in and of itself holds categories as its norms and could not do any more than just work as the schemata, it now gains positivity; and so long as it does not deviate from the lawfulness of understanding in general, it can demonstrate its free play. The creation of artistic genius also takes place here. Imagination, in this manner, becomes positive for the first time in feelings and as freedom gains practical realness (実在性) in the world of ethical will, we would have to say that it is licensed here with aesthetic realness (美的実在性). Now, what does it mean to say that understanding and imagination, as that which constitutes feelings, are tied to each other in its universality (一般)? If this universal should be interpreted as the mere abstract one that externally negates the particular and abandons it, what would happen? In that case, feeling merely as the faculty of general pleasure (一般的快の能力) has no choice but to become that which has lost the possibility of particularization in every sense of the word. Thus, Kant has attributed the rich creativity of the aesthetic representation (美的表象) of genius—which he calls aesthetic ideal—to imagination above everything else. If that is the case, then we would have to say that imagination in general cannot be the abstract universal. It would have to be the faculty (能力) that can actively produce aesthetic representation from inside itself as the concrete universal. The feeling in this sense as the universal that, *so to speak*, includes all particulars within itself must be precisely the unity of understanding and imagination. Then, that which includes all particulars would have to transcend them at the limit of the series of these particulars. Not only as that which transcends [particulars], but also as that which differentiates [itself from] all the particulars as its self-determination, such a thing would have to be at the same time "acting" (働くもの) or precisely the act (作用). Now, in Kant, understanding and imagination would have to be theoretical, insofar as the former acts towards the particular (特殊的に働き) as the categories that correspond with various forms of the judgment of general logic, and the latter insofar as it works in the manner of the particular in response to these categories. Then, we must say that feelings appear to be established when understanding that works theoretically and objectively, and imagination, namely the faculties of cognition (認識能力), transcend themselves towards the foundation of their intellectual functions and increase its profoundness in this process of trans-descendance. The feeling in this manner is established at the standpoint where it transdescends and subsumes intellect. Hence, this is precisely why a single rose can be an object of knowledge in one aspect, but at the same time it could further transcend this [aspect] in its profound depth, where it is embraced by feelings, it is given to us as the beautiful, and as that which should be musically praised by poets through many aesthetic representations. At this moment, because the faculty of cognition (認識能力) transcends this particular determination and becomes the "universal," that is to say, theoretically speaking, it acts "without determinations," the judgment of feeling itself adds nothing to the theoretical significance of object; and the aesthetic judgment in this manner takes non-conceptuality as one of its essential characters. Kant calls the unity between understanding and imagination in this kind of universality the "supersensible substance of humanity" (op. cit. 237). Since it is the universality that transdescends theoretical and particular determination, it must give the infinitely rich and aesthetic power of creativity rather as the profound and fundamental act of the dynamic production as previously mentioned. We can say that Cassirer's statement that this supersensible substance is "the fundamental function of the spiritual" accurately captures the high dimensionality and fundamentality of feeling. The supersensible substance of humanity is in fact the feeling subject (感情的主体). It is not only the subject of aesthetic contemplation but at the same time, as Kant himself says (op. cit. 242), it has to be the principle of genius as the faculty of aesthetic creation. The inner of artistic expression in Kant has no choice but to be feeling in this sense.

It is not our main concern here to reflect on various ideas in the works of Kant. What I have shown so far is that I focused on the section where he clarified the structure of the feeling of the beautiful and succinctly reflected on his idea of beauty. However, because of this, I believe we have been able to sufficiently pay due attention to how he has laid out a suggestive passage towards our insight, the insight that the standpoint of pure feeling is not simply established as something abstract but rather established when the subject continuously cultivates its depth at the bottom of all life-content that shapes humanity. Now, non-conceptuality and disinterestedness were as we have seen above the negative characteristics of pure feeling. They precisely show the discontinuity and transcendence, as well as high dimensionality and concreteness, of pure feeling vis-à-vis the intellect and that which pertains to will. In this way, Schopenhauer moved from the disinterestedness of beauty in Kant's aesthetics to the world of aesthetic enlightenment (解脱). The term "disinterestedness" precisely means a discontinuation and a transcendence of all that has to do with desire; and the beauty therein promises the world of liberation from human suffering in its entirety. Also, in this case, the world of desire is not absorbed into the shadow of its extinction but subsumed as it is being transcended at the disinterested standpoint, and it is quietly contemplated through the undisturbed mind. Schiller has also developed the highest ideal for human formation by similarly starting from disinterestedness in Kantian aesthetics and by moving in the direction of its higher dimensionality and concreteness. The mission of human existence lies in the development from a human being as a natural being to a moral being. The character of humans as a natural being is of course sensible (感性的) and appetitive (欲求的), and contrariwise, their essential character as a moral being is rational and complies with the law without being obstructed by desires. Human beings are essentially the contradictory existence of the sensible and the rational. Accordingly, the natural and the rational always struggle against each other inside us, and regardless of the fact that the rational orders us from duty, its realization is always obstructed by the sensible. Therefore, because beauty takes disinterestedness as its essential characteristic, it frees humans from sensible desires and hence, places them in a state where there is no obstacle from being rational and lawful. In this sense, beauty for Schiller would have to be a stage of the mediatory process that stands between the natural and the moral, and facilitates the transition between them. However, he further pursues the significance of aesthetic character in a more profound fashion. As we have clarified above, in Kant, beauty is established in the harmony between freedom of imagination and lawfulness of understanding. If we understand the fundamental idea of Schiller's philosophy in relation to this, [we would say] he understood the essence of beauty in the harmony between the principle of sensibility and the principle of rationality. If we think about the fact that imagination is also the principle of concrete sensible intuition in Kant, not only does that understanding belong to a part of reason in the broad sense, but also that the structure of noble beauty is demonstrated through the unity of imagination and the (moral) reason, and there is no principal impossibility in the relevancy of Schiller to Kant. Now, if beauty is established through the harmony of the sensible and the rational in this manner, it means that it is established in the concrete union of both, and also, accordingly, that it is naturally even higher than these two as the unity of things that are essentially contradictory or in opposition to each other. Therefore, if we move from this standpoint to action (行爲), this action must spontaneously be in accordance with the law of reason. Not only is moral action unobstructed by the natural and the sensible here, but through harmonizing itself with them, it is fully actualized as the content of abundant life, thereby revealing the world of expression of humanity as a whole (全

人間性) that we ought not to lose. Here, the natural does not receive any obligation from reason and the latter is not resisted by the former; both will form a beautiful act (行爲) as the synthetic unity between the fulfilling content of life and the form of reason as the good; the heart-and-mind (心) as it flows, the act as it comes to be, [they are] natural and yet also do not depart from the good. Thus, the act here transcends the character of oughtness as described in Kantian ethics and enters the world of "play." In play, namely in beauty, a human lives its humanity as a whole in its complete form for the first time. "A human being, where he plays, only there is wholistically human" (Über *die* ästhetische *Erziehung des menschen, Vierzehnter Brief*). Therefore, we can say that the morality of oughtness is transcended by the idea of beauty in Schiller's work. However, the simple act of goodness still does not escape abstraction. Wholistic humanity expresses itself only in a "beautiful act" (美しき行爲) which comes from the "beautiful soul." The human formation holds the highest goal in such soul.

It may appear at a glance that my investigation has slightly deviated from the main concern of this chapter. What is the artistic and expressive inner? This was the problem we were thinking about. If it is acceptable to think about human life by dividing it into intellect (知) and feeling-and-will (情意), aesthetic feeling cannot be a mere abstract pleasure at all but rather it is established where it trans-descends intellect and will, and by negating them inside itself, it affirms and assimilates them (摂収する). In this manner, we have thought about the issue. In this sense, there cannot be any intellect or will that cannot be aesthetic content. Of course, knowledge (知識) or will in itself cannot possibly carry the aesthetic meaning. Additionally, when they come to be purified towards the world of pure feeling that consists of non-conceptuality and disinterestedness, all desires and knowledge are subsumed into the higher dimensional world of beauty. We can say that in this sense beauty is the wholistic and absolute affirmation of the content of all life. The inner of artistic expression must be the feeling in this sense. —Indeed, the feelings that are directly tied to desire and intellect are rather the objective feelings as that which is noematic in the abovementioned sense, it would have to be clear in relation to that which we have demonstrated so far, that it is the opposite of aesthetic feeling.

When we say "feelings," people might quickly point out its direct-ness or immediacy. Also, because of that, they might rigorously enquire how it can be granted with high dimensionality which essentially presupposes mediation. The feeling, indeed, is immediate. However, life is originally mediatory, and I wonder if there is no moment that is not mediatory in concrete life. Some might ask how simple sensation (感覚) is possible. However, I wonder if simple sensation, which is thought in the field of psychology, is in fact an abstraction based on speculation, and also if in reference to the experience of concrete life, a mere sensation, hovering in the air, without having any characteristics does not exist anywhere. Sensation is probably the simplest structure established in the dialectical mediation between the subject and the opposite. Is it not in such mediation, that the entanglement of representations is sublated to the concept, thereby giving birth to (academic) studies? Isn't the world of practice established where we severe the intellectual struggle that cannot be ultimately dissolved at the standpoint of intellect through the act (行為) and sublation of it towards the act? If we think that intellect can discriminately judge all things human and that the act is a business that is divisible by the intellect, is it not extreme overconfidence in intellect and ridiculously naïve optimism against the complexity of existence that is called a human being? Even in the abstract world of numbers, what discovers the irrational numbers is the human being. All struggles of life, joy and sadness, grudge and reconciliation—all these things are sublated towards the purified, infinite abyss—isn't that where the aesthetic feeling flows? The feeling is indeed immediate. However, is its immediacy—which might sound like a paradox—an immediacy that transcends mediation? Feeling swallows up (併呑している) the mediation. When we say that a number of feelings and thoughts come forth one after another (万感交に起こる), or that we are overwhelmed with deep emotions (感慨無量), can this be the immediacy that negates and excludes the activity (働き) of intellect and will? Rather, is it not the case that intellect and will in their entirety are exhaustively performing their act therein? The ultimacy of intellect and will, and the infinite that transcends and embraces the intellect and will therein, that is precisely the feeling as the inner in the artistic expression.

Feeling as the inner in artistic expression is immediate in the abovementioned sense, and further has the *omomuki* (おもむき).[5] It is said that since in opposition to *somuki* (そむき), which derives from the term "turning away from" or "turning our backs to" (背向き) [something], the *omomuki* derives from "turning towards" or "facing towards" (面向く) [something]. This shows that the term should mean a movement towards a certain direction and then, signifies the essence (こころ) or reason of things and events, and namely their intent (趣意), and further signifies their free state of being (好き有り様). The term "taste" (趣味) precisely indicates the natural characteristics (持ち味) in the things-and-events' free state of being. Hence, perhaps we can say the following: *omomuki* is to be in the movement (動向) where a certain meaning, which directly expresses self in its free state of being, advocates itself. The inner in artistic expression is nothing but this kind of movement of the subject (主体). In this sense, it is appropriate for us to refer to this as "mood(s)" (*jōshu* 情趣).[6] When we use the term *jōsho* (情緒),[7] *sho* originally means the clue or the beginning of things (糸口), and *jōsho* signifies the beginning of the movement of the heart-and-mind (*kokoro*) and the cross-section where emotions (心情) are brought forth. In this case, even though *jōsho* positively expresses the dynamic characteristic of feelings (*jōsho*), it indicates a static state as emotions' way of being: hence, regarding this point, we have to say, it is insufficient. Contrariwise, *Stimmung* is the term that rather indicates emotions' state of affairs (有り様), and which does not express *omomuki* as its development (動勢). In opposition to this, the English term "emotion", which is usually given as the translation of *jōsho*, originates from the term *emovère*, which means to move and shake, and from there, it came to mean intense excitement and profound emotion of the heart (心), which does not at all match *Stimmung* in that

---

5   [This term could mean "taste" as in 趣, but since Kimura writes it in hiragana and uses a different expression 面向き which literally means "facing towards [us]" as opposed to "facing away [from us]" as in 背向き, the expression should be understood to imply multiple meanings. In order to maintain the ambiguity and avoid reducing it to a single meaning, we have decided to leave the term untranslated.]

6   [Ordinarily, 情趣 in Japanese refers to a "profound taste and sensitivity of things" and that is also what is meant by the technical term, "mood(s)," here.]

7   [which means a certain profound taste or sensible aspects of things that can bring about various feelings.]

the latter can accept the deep and quiet tune of the heart's string. This word originally meant the emission of voice (*Stimme*) and the attunement of musical instruments. It came to signify the state of heart-and-mind and its mood (気分) by probably just moving the tune [from the voice] to the string of *kokoro*. We can easily see the linguistic significance of this term, *Stimmung*, in Kant's works. When he thinks the judgment of taste is established as the aesthetic judgment, because a representation provides the "proportional *Stimmung*" (*proponierte Stimmung*) to the faculty of cognition, what is said here as the faculty of cognition is nothing but the previously mentioned imagination and understanding. When saying that beauty is judged in *jōsho* accordance with the "purposive *Stimmung*/tuning of imagination in its correspondence (Übereinstimmung) with the faculty of concept in general,"[8] when imagination and the faculty of concept in general, namely understanding, literally harmonize their voices and overlap with each other (übereinstimmen), where they spontaneously harmonize each of their characteristics with the other without harming it, the purposive attunement between them is established; thus, Kant says, this is precisely the feeling of the beautiful. In other words, the tuning between two strings of the heart (i.e., imagination and understanding), this *Stimmung* preserves the "animation of inner relationships" (*inneres Verhältnis zur Belebung*) (p. 66), namely the interrelation of internal ratio, and such animated "tuning" (*Stimmung*) cannot give any determination (*bestimmen*) without relying on feelings (*Gefühl*)" (*ibid*)—this is how Kant puts it. Where this "relation" is "felt,"— "sensitive relationship" (*empfindares Verhältnis*) (152)—namely where the immediate experience of this relation is established—the feeling of beauty is born. The beautiful is precisely that which is established based on "a merely sensible relationship between imagination and understanding, which are mutually attuned to the form of the object" (*ein bloss empfindbares Verhältnis der an der vorgestellten Form des Objekts wechselseitig untereinander stimmenden Einbildungskraft und des Verstandes* [ibid]). —If we trace this line of thinking in this way, we have to say that Kant's *Stimmung* clearly shows its insight into the way of *kokoro*'s *omomuki*, which we have called *jōshu*, in its hidden

---

8   Op. cit., 242.

depth, and comprehends it well. The tune that the heartstrings play is *jōshu*. *Jōshu* is the already felt heart-and-mind, already revealed heart inside itself, and the heart that has manifested itself toward itself. In this sense, we have to say that *jōshu* is already the internal expression of subject itself and its internal formation. If *jōshu* as the inner of artistic expression is precisely the tune played by the heartstrings that form the human subject, then it should be naturally discerned that a mere individual feeling should not be immediately entitled as the inner in artistic expression. The content of *jōshu* must be the life of "humans." Thus, the human is not an individual. Nor is it a mere group of individuals. The individual is rather nothing but the individual of the human. The feeling of the mere individual is contingent and we cannot say that it is rooted in what Kant calls the "supersensible substance of human beings." Feeling that has lost universality as human experience cannot be the content of art in any sense. That is why, for example, T. S. Eliot says—"[poetry] is not the expression of personality but rather an escape from personality."[9] However, does art then aim at pale universality? That would have to be the business of abstract studies. What kind of universality is that which the inner in artistic expression has? Perhaps we will find an opportunity to answer this question later.

The inner in artistic expression is *jōshu* as the manifestation of the innerness of human life in the abovementioned sense. Now, *jōshu* is the heart-and-minds' way of being and its condition; and at the same time, it is a turning towards a single direction. It is essentially mobile being (動向的な存在). Where does it turn towards? —Indeed here the problem concerning the form of art is established. A movement in *jōshu* is neither a mere movement of emotions, nor a mere transition, nor even a simple change, but progress towards a certain direction. *Jōshu* is originally the play of the heart's strings. That which is rhythmical can live there. That which seems to have form can live there. That which is temporal and that which is spatial can live in its internally indeterminate way of being—or rather, therein lies an indication of the birth of time and space.

---

9   T.S. Eliot, *Tradition and the Individual Talent.*

NOTES ON CONTRIBUTORS

ONUR KARAMERCAN is an independent scholar, currently based in Paris, France. His doctoral thesis at the University of Tasmania examined Heidegger's topological thought of language, dwelling and place. He spent research periods at the University of Crete and University at Buffalo (SUNY). Specialized in 20th century hermeneutic phenomenology, his work engages with literary and philosophical questions related to the study of space and place. His most recent work includes *Locating Heidegger's kotoba between Actuality and Hollowness: The Way Towards a Thinking Conversation with Japanese Philosophy*. The Journal of East Asian Philosophy, Springer (forthcoming); *Heidegger's Way to Poetic Dwelling via Being and Time*. Horizon: Studies in Phenomenology, 10 (1), 2021, 268–285; *Could Humans Dwell Beyond the Earth? Thinking with Heidegger on Space Colonization and the Topology of Technology*. Interdisciplinary Studies in Literature and Environment, 2021, 1–26.

TAKESHI MORISATO currently serves as the editor of the *European Journal of Japanese Philosophy* (EJJP), the book series "Studies in Japanese Philosophy" (Nagoya: Chisokudō Publications) and "Asian Philosophical Texts" (Milan: Mimesis International). Additionally, he works as the regional editor of the "Bloomsbury Introduction to World Philosophies" (London: Bloomsbury) and the associate editor of the *Journal of East Asian Philosophy* (New York: Springer). His previous publications include, *Faith and Reason in Continental and Japanese Philosophy* (London: Bloomsbury, 2019), and his research interests are in metaphysics, philosophy of religion, the Kyoto School, metaxology, and world philosophies.

Rossa Ó Muireartaigh is an associate professor at the School of Foreign Studies, Aichi Prefectural University, Japan. His research includes the philosophy of the Kyoto School, in particular the writings of D.T. Suzuki. He has also worked in the area of the philosophy of translation and is the author of the book *Begotten, Not Made: Explorations in the Philosophy and Sociology of Religious Translation* (Atropos Press, 2015). He is currently completing a book on the philosophy of D.T. Suzuki.

Roman Paşca is an assistant professor at the Department of Japanese Philosophy at Kyoto University's Graduate School of Letters. He currently serves as vice-president of the European Network of Japanese Philosophy (ENOJP) and as a book review editor for the *European Journal of Japanese Philosophy*. His research focuses on the development of the concept of "nature" in premodern Japanese philosophy, especially in the works of Edo period philosophers like Andō Shōeki, Yamagata Bantō, Ishida Baigan, Ninomiya Sontoku, etc. He is also working on the relation between nature and self within the frame of environmental ethics, and on "deep ecology" in Japanese philosophy.

Kyle Michael James Shuttleworth (Rikkyo University) is a JSPS International Research Fellow, currently working on environmental ethics and Japanese philosophy. He has previously taught at Queen's University Belfast, The Royal Institute of Philosophy, and Japan Women's University. His research interests include modern ethical ideals, the thought of Watsuji Tetsurō, and the ethical interface between Japanese and continental philosophy. He has published in each of these areas, including research papers and translations in *Asian Philosophy* and *Philosophy East and West*, and a monograph, *The History and Ethics of Authenticity* (2020), with Bloomsbury. He is also an editor for the interdisciplinary journal *Philosophy and Cultural Embodiment*.

TAISUKE UENO is a lecturer at the Faculty of Global Liberal Arts at Kanda University of International Studies. He is currently working on "Japanized" ethics and ethics in the intellectual history of Japan (*Rinrigaku* or *Nihon-Rinrishisōshi*). His research interests include Zeami's performance theory, *Hagakure*, the methodology of "Japanized" ethics since Watsuji Tetsurō, and the essence of ordinary life of human beings. His recent publications include the book *Hana tsutou hana: Zeami densho no shisō* [Transmission from Flower to Flower] (Kyōto: Kōyō Shobō, 2017), contributions to the most recent annotated edition of *Hagakure* (Tōkyō: Chikuma Shobo, 2017), and the article *On Jōchō's Suffering through Survival: "I Have Found the Way of the Warrior in Death"* (2020).

YIHSOONG YU received his PhD in philosophy at the Sun-Yat-Sen University in 2017. His specialization is Chinese Philosophy and he published articles both in English and Chinese on various topics concerning Neo-Confucian philosophy. His previous publications include "Stephen Angle's Notion of Coherence," Philosophy East and West, 71 (2021): 241–259.

DIANA YÜKSEL is an associate professor of Korean language and literature at the University of Bucharest. She studied East Asian philosophy at Yonsei University in Seoul and was a visiting scholar with the Korea Institute at Harvard University. Her main field of research is Confucianism in Korea, with a focus on notions such as moral duty, moral norms and moral self-accomplishment. She has also published Korean language learning materials, and translated several works of contemporary Korean literature.

Printed by
Digital Team – Fano (PU)
September 2021